The Power
of a
Covenant Heart

The Power
of a
Covenant Heart

Bishop David R. Huskins

Image of Jesus on cover courtesy of Holy Transfiguration Monastery.

Destiny Image® Publishers, Inc.
P.O. Box 310
Shippensburg, PA 17257-0310

"We Publish the Prophets"

ISBN 0-7684-2116-0

For Worldwide Distribution
Printed in the U.S.A.

3 4 5 6 7 8 9 10 11 12 13 / 10 09 08 06 05

This book and all other Destiny Image, Revival Press,
MercyPlace, Fresh Bread, Destiny Image Fiction,
and Treasure House books are available
at Christian bookstores and distributors worldwide.

For a U.S. bookstore nearest you, call **1-800-722-6774**.
For more information on foreign distributors, call **717-532-3040**.
Or reach us on the Internet: **www.destinyimage.com**

Dedication

God has indeed been better to me than I have been to myself. His greatest gifts and treasures are those packaged in earthen vessels. No other treasure has been more valuable to me than the God-sent treasure of John Huskins, my father.

John Huskins was a man of little education, yet one who was so very wise. Notwithstanding humble beginnings, he convinced my brother and me that wealth was not restricted to income and bank accounts. Rather, true wealth was about character and integrity.

My father, John Huskins, waited until just two years before his death to surrender to the lordship of Jesus Christ. Yet throughout his life, he modeled *The Power of a Covenant Heart*. His word was sure and could be counted on in every situation. He married once, believing that the covenant of marriage should be once and forever.

Daddy took covenant seriously. He never spoke evil of anyone. He would treat an enemy with the same respect with which he would treat a friend. He was a man of honor.

My father's graduation to a higher realm of life left a deep void throughout my entire family. Daddy was gone. John Huskins may be gone, but he is certainly not forgotten.

In the words of a popular poem:

I got it from my father,
It was all he had to give.
It is mine to use and cherish,
For as long as I may live.

I can lose the natural gifts he gave me,
And they can be replaced,
But a black mark on my name
Can never be erased.

It was clean the day I took it
And a worthy name to bear.
When he got it from my grandfather,
There was no dishonor there.

I have guarded it wisely
Because after all is said and done,
I must be sure it is spotless
As I give it to my sons.

(Source unknown)

I dedicate this book to the memory of the name of:

John A. Huskins,
the man who had *a covenant heart*.

Acknowledgments

To those who are my greatest credentials: my wife, Michelle, and my three sons, Aaron, Zach, and Isaac. You sacrifice daily to allow me to pursue the mission and vision of a covenant heart. I love you all unconditionally and totally.

To Dr. Kenneth Meadors, for his special assistance in preparing the text of this book and for his wisdom through the years. A part of you will always be in me.

To Pastor Kelley Varner, for inspiring and encouraging me to write this volume, and for helping me to edit the final manuscript. I am even more grateful for our friendship.

To the great saints of Cedar Lake Christian Center: Without you, I would know little of covenant. Through the years, we have grown and learned together. I am a covenant man today because of you. The best is still yet to come.

To all the pastors, churches, and ministries who have opened their hearts and lives to me: I can never thank you enough for your relationship. The Lord be between us forever.

To every Jonathan and David (you know who you are) who has ever touched my life or allowed me to touch your life: May we never take for granted what God has joined together.

To my spiritual father, Archbishop Earl Paulk, who is the epitome of a man of covenant: All of my days are committed to faithfully serving you and the vision you have imparted.

Contents

Foreword

The first time I saw David Huskins, I pondered in my heart how a man of his youth could have gone so far in the work of the Kingdom in such a short time. He was called a bishop, and my thought was, "a bishop over what?" (This was before I got to know David Huskins or the actual extent of his labors.)

It did not take long for me to discover that he was indeed a special anointed vessel of God. I was invited to speak to his network of churches over which he is bishop. As time went along, he began to minister some in the Cathedral here in Atlanta. I was with him in many sessions that required great wisdom in the International Communion of Charismatic Churches. I found out that God had granted him great wisdom and understanding far beyond his natural years.

I was to learn sometime later that I had had the joy of helping to birth him into the knowledge of the gospel of the Kingdom. The first time that he called me his spiritual father, there was an immediate bonding. Now he is truly a son of mine, and I trust him immeasurably.

When I read his book, *The Power of a Covenant Heart*, I realized it was his spiritual understanding that had brought him the tremendous success that he enjoys. He recognizes not only our vertical covenant relationship with God, but also our horizontal covenant with the Church and its leadership. This book is filled with Scripture-based, beautifully written, and enjoyable writings.

I strongly suggest that you read this book and share it with others. It will definitely enhance your life.

Archbishop Earl Paulk

Introduction

Covenant—the mere mention of this word brings forth all kinds of emotions from all kinds of people. A person's concept of covenant depends upon his or her background, previous teaching, and church experiences, both positive and negative.

To most, *covenant* means a mutual agreement between two or more parties. That definition is good, but limited, for it could just as adequately apply to *contract* as well as *covenant*.

There is a major difference between a contract and a covenant. By nature, contracts are legal and binding. Covenants are spiritual and liberating. Contracts are sealed on paper. Covenants are sealed in the heart. Covenants are more binding than contracts. The essential difference is that a contract is enforced by the law, and a covenant is enforced by the spirit.

When the Holy Spirit first captured my attention and said to me, "I have called you to establish covenantal relationships that cannot be broken," I had no idea what they were or how to begin to establish them. The Lord then took me to the Old Testament scriptural story of David and Jonathan. For the last 12 years of my life, this story has served as a pattern or prototype of what I believe true covenant is all about. It is from that backdrop of scriptural passages that we will launch our journey into the wonderful world of unbreakable relationships.

Covenant works essentially in two dimensions, two dynamics. Primarily, it involves our personal relationship with God. That subject has been given much attention throughout Christendom. However, covenant also involves our relationship with each other, which has been almost completely ignored in the Body of Christ. It is the latter dimension that we will explore together in the pages that follow.

Covenant is not only a relational word; it is also a redemptive word. The Redemption Covenant deserves and should be given a complete study of its own. If it were not for the Covenant of Redemption, all other covenants would be of no value. If properly understood, every covenant—from salvation to marriage to church membership—flows intrinsically from the eternal covenant cut intertheistically between the Father and the Son. The Father as Creator was inseparable from the Son as Redeemer. Covenants in redemption and relationships are and were sealed by blood. The blood of the Son sealed the New Covenant.

Likewise, it is important to establish *covenant* as an eschatological word. Most believers usually view last things from one of two perspectives—from a traditional dispensational point of view, or from a more correct historical and covenantal point of view. If God began His involvement with man and Israel by covenant, then proper laws of interpretation would mandate that He would consummate that involvement by covenant. If the beginnings of God's dealings with man and Israel were determined by times and portions, then one could conclude that God is dispensational. Unfortunately, obedience and covenant would have little real significance in such an endtime philosophy. To me, the dispensational view has become reckless, absurd, and impractical. God has always demanded covenantal obedience.

As exciting as the redemptive and eschatological studies would be, my focus and thrust in this treatise shall be personally and practically relational. What happens when God supernaturally knits your soul with another member of the Body of Christ? Why does God join you to others? How do we recognize our covenant brother or sister? What makes a covenant brother or sister different from the rest of the household of faith? Should every one have a covenant brother or sister?

In a day when relationships are discarded for the smallest of excuses, Christians must demonstrate the gospel through covenantal relationships that cannot be broken. In the first chapter of Romans, the apostle Paul lists the progression of becoming reprobate in mind. He states in verse 31, "Without understanding, covenantbreakers, without natural affection, implacable, unmerciful." The word *covenantbreakers* means "not agreed, treacherous to compacts, not keeping covenant."

This verse gives great insight into the present strategy of the enemy against the people of God. If saints remain ignorant of their covenants, they will consequently break them. Such unnatural affections will then produce a stubborn (implacable), unmerciful Church.

I want to remedy that. After we have taken together a fresh look at the covenantal model of David and Jonathan, I hope we can say, "With understanding we are covenant keepers that are flexible and full of mercy."

Through covenant, God partners with men and women in order that we may fulfill His eternal purposes in earth as it is in Heaven. He performs this in two ways—by joining Himself to His creation, and by knitting members of His creation to each other.

For there is one God, and one mediator between God and men, the man Christ Jesus (1 Timothy 2:5).

This verse is usually quoted to say that there is one mediator between God and "man." That is still true, for there is no other name whereby we can be saved. Jesus Christ is mankind's only Savior (see Jn. 14:6; Acts 4:12). But this passage refers to mediation between God and "men."

The man Christ Jesus is the only One in the middle of our relationship with God. He is also the One in the middle of our relationships with each other. This truth of horizontal mediation is why David and Jonathan vowed, "The Lord be between me and thee, and between my seed and thy seed forever" (1 Sam. 20:42b). Jesus is in the middle of our vertical relationship with God. We must allow Him to mediate all our horizontal relationships as well. May the Lord be between us.

It is with this desire that we look at the covenant between David and Jonathan. It is a pattern, though it may not be a perfect one. As with David and Jonathan's relationship, all covenant relationships will be tested. This testing comes in the form of the choices that we make. This very important part of covenantal life reveals just how committed we are to being covenant keepers. God never breaks His portion of the covenant. The challenge is for each of us to keep our end of the covenant with God and with each other.

Come with me now as we journey with David, the man after God's own heart. Each stage of his life reveals another piece of the covenant heart. Note that the New Testament apostolic models of Jesus and Paul end each section.

As we move into the new Millennium, the enemy's greatest fear is that the Church will grow up and build unbreakable covenant relationships against which he has no power. The thing he fears is about to come upon him, because we are no longer insecure and arrogant. We are now secure and humble enough to lose ourselves in someone else. *The Power of a Covenant Heart* is unstoppable. Let us find ourselves in someone else!

Bishop David R. Huskins

Chapter One

Covenant People Will Never Leave the Sheep Unprotected

Our covenant prototype David is introduced in the Bible as a young and ruddy keeper of the sheep. It is this involvement with the sheep that distinguishes him from his seven other brethren. When Samuel prepares to anoint a king among the sons of Jesse, he is given specific instructions not to look upon their countenance or the height of their stature because God is looking upon the heart.

Jesse does not feel that David even qualifies for consideration. While his natural father sees but a shepherd boy, his heavenly Father sees the power of a covenant heart that will qualify him to be king over a greater flock. God has always chosen men and women with a covenant heart.

And Samuel said unto Jesse, Are here all thy children? And he said, There remaineth yet the youngest, and, behold, he keepeth the sheep. And Samuel said unto Jesse, Send and fetch him: for we will not sit down till he come hither. And he sent, and brought him in. Now he was ruddy, and withal of a beautiful

1

*countenance, and goodly to look to. And the Lord said, Arise,
anoint him: for this is he* (1 Samuel 16:11-12).

❦ ⸙⸙⸙⸙ ❦

Sadly, here in America, the particular platforms an individual
may stand on, or the number of crowds following his or her ministry, have been used as the determinate measure of his or her success. While that may have some importance to some men and
women, it has little or no value to God. Faithfulness, integrity, and
character mark his measuring stick. God always checks to see if His
man or woman can keep and maintain covenant. He is not interested in how many ministries we can start, but rather how many
we can be faithful to until the work is finished.

David did not seek to promote himself. He kept the flock until
he was called for. The words *remaineth* and *keepeth* in First Samuel
16:11 are both covenantal words. *Remaineth* comes from the
Hebrew word *sha'ar* (Strongs #7604), which means the "reserve or
remnant." God is reserving a faithful remnant who will keep
covenant with the flock of God until He calls for them.

Keepeth is the Hebrew word *ra'ah* (Strong's #7462), and it
means "to tend, rule or associate as a companion, friend, pastor
and to keep company with." There are faithful keepers who will
tend to the flock of God and rule the congregation, not with a rod
of iron, but through covenant relationships. Do not be afraid to
touch people, to get close to the sheep. Every real shepherd will
have the smell of sheep on them somewhere.

The trend today among many ministers is to remain with a
congregation until a better door of opportunity comes along.
Their attitude is one of self-promotion instead of corporate destiny. Many preachers still do not understand that their gifting is
not for themselves, but rather for the sheep.

David began his ministry, not in the spotlight, but in the
moonlight, taking care of the sheep. God said to Samuel, "Arise,

anoint him: for this is he" (1 Sam. 16:12b). This reveals the first principle of being a covenant person: *Covenant people will never leave the sheep unprotected.*

God cares for the sheep. David skipped the big ordination and consecration service to take care of the sheep. It was only after God rejected the glitter and glamour guys that Bishop Samuel asked if there were any other sons. God anointed the young, ruddy sheep-keeper above his brethren. While they were practicing their smiles and polishing their skills for the television camera, David was fighting off bears and lions to protect the sheep.

God is still looking for shepherds who are more interested in the sheep than their own personal success. Apprehended ones fully realize that God is aware of them in the field, and know that He will call for them when He is ready. These are not posturing for position, knowing that they already hold the highest position in the land—they are shepherds! David was a shepherd.

When God was ready to announce the birth of His Son Jesus, He did not first appear unto wise men. He appeared unto simple country shepherds, who were "abiding in [their] field" (Lk. 2:8). *Abiding* is another covenantal term. To quote the title of a modern movie, covenant is about *The Terms of Endearment.* Can we abide in the place of our calling? Will we stick together when the going gets tough?

The Greek root word for "abiding" is similar to the previously mentioned Hebrew word used for "keepeth" in First Samuel 16:11, confirming this covenantal principle in both the Old and New Testaments. *Abiding* can also be linked to the word *remaining,* which deals with the remnant. The remnant is not some small elite group. The remnant is that which is left after all else has fallen by the way of all flesh. Let us be found abiding in covenant when others have broken covenant.

The shepherds in Luke 2:8 were not only abiding; they were keeping watch "over" their flock by night. As shepherds, our role is not to look at the flock, but to watch over them. If God has given you *over*sight, He has also given you night vision. During seasons of darkness in which the lives of your flock abide, keep watch over them until you see the light that dawns on their behalf.

This first principle is applicable not only for pastoral shepherds; it also works for parents of children, for husbands who are willing to be the priests of their homes, and for employers who are willing to conduct business by the Word of God.

Covenantal people never use the flock to advance themselves. Covenant people will lay down their lives to advance the flock.

Church membership has almost become a one-night stand in America. Some people change churches as often as the season changes. This problem plagues preachers as well. As soon as a bigger opportunity or a little fame and fortune come along, pastors divorce the (spiritual) woman of their youth to pursue another. That other "woman," part of a popular system, gives them instant gratification. Unfortunately, it happens at the expense of the people who have loved and supported them through the early night seasons of their life and ministry.

David left the sheepfold and journeyed on to many famous events, including the obtaining of great wealth, but he never betrayed the sheep. After being chosen to minister as King Saul's armorbearer, he walked away from the excitement of the palace and returned to Bethlehem to feed his father's sheep. When David engaged in the conflict with Goliath, he left the sheep with a keeper.

And David rose up early in the morning, and left the sheep with a keeper... (1 Samuel 17:20).

David's eldest brother, who knew his commitment to the sheep, mocked him by asking "...with whom hast thou left those few sheep in the wilderness?" (1 Sam. 17:28a). A covenant shepherd never leaves the sheep unprotected, especially when they are in the wilderness. Moreover, "David left his carriage in the hand of the keeper of the carriage" (1 Sam. 17:22a). God honors keepers of covenant. *Covenant people will never leave the sheep unprotected* or in the hands of hirelings. That is what real shepherds understand.

What Eliab, David's oldest brother, did not understand (by looking at the numbers of David's flock) is that God was focused on David's commitment to the flock. God does not disqualify seed; rather, He qualifies it. What disqualified David in Eliab's thinking is precisely what qualified David in God's mind. *He was a keeper of the sheep.*

How many today would leave some famous mega-ministry platform to return to feed a congregation of a couple of hundred faithful parishioners? Many would consider it below their dignity to do such a thing. Yet God still honors those who are willing to blossom where they are planted. David understood that whatever he ultimately accomplished was primarily a result of his time spent with his "few" sheep.

Covenant people will never leave the sheep unprotected. Pastors, you have a covenant with your flock. Husbands and wives, you have a covenant with each other. Parents, you have a covenant with your children. Employers, you have a covenant with your employees. Go out and come in as you must, but never at the expense of leaving the sheep unprotected.

I have been blessed by God to stand in some of the greatest and largest pulpits in our nation and abroad. All of the largest are not necessarily the greatest, and all of the greatest are not necessarily the largest. Nonetheless, my marriage to a congregation of several hundred faithful people in a small rural northwest Georgia community of several thousand is still where my vows and heart will always remain. *The sheep* of Cedar Lake Christian Center *are never left unprotected.*

There is no greater test of a covenant heart than to see if you are willing to abide in the field where God has planted you, to see if you will keep watch (remain consistent) over the flock God has given you. If you remain steadfast, God will prosper you to reach many higher dimensions. Moreover, He will prosper your flock to reach those levels of blessing and promotion with you. Be faithful with the small things, and the really big things in your life will come. Despise not the days of small beginnings (see Zech. 4:10).

A covenant-keeping shepherd will have a covenant-keeping congregation. It may begin small, but you cannot keep a covenant family from growing. Remember, mere numbers alone do not determine growth in God. Growth is determined by the sphere of influence your covenant family exemplifies in the earth. Because *David never left the sheep unprotected,* his world of influence grew and grew.

The apostle Paul understood like David that the proof of your ministry is the sheepfold you keep. He declared, "If I be not an apostle unto others, yet doubtless I am to you: for the seal of mine apostleship are ye in the Lord" (1 Cor. 9:2). It really has little to do with how many congregations or families we can start, but instead how faithful we are to keep covenant with the ones we have.

Old Testament Covenant Scriptures

David Was Committed to the Flock

There remaineth yet the youngest, and, behold, he keepeth the sheep.

Wherefore Saul sent messengers unto Jesse, and said, Send me David thy son, which is with the sheep.

And David came to Saul, and stood before him: and he loved him greatly; and he became his armourbearer (1 Samuel 16:11b,19,21).

David Never Left the Sheep Unprotected

But David went and returned from Saul to feed his father's sheep at Bethlehem.

And David rose up early in the morning, and left the sheep with a keeper, and took, and went, as Jesse had commanded him....

And David left his carriage in the hand of the keeper of the carriage....

...and with whom hast thou left those few sheep in the wilderness? (1 Samuel 17:15,20,22,28a).

New Testament Applications

Jesus Never Left the Sheep Unprotected

I am the good shepherd: the good shepherd giveth His life for the sheep.

But he that is an hireling, and not the shepherd, whose own the sheep are not, seeth the wolf coming, and leaveth the sheep, and fleeth: and the wolf catcheth them, and scattereth the sheep (John 10:11-12).

Paul Never Left the Sheep Unprotected

And when they had ordained them elders in every church, and had prayed with fasting, they commended them to the Lord, on whom they believed (Acts 14:23).

And some days after Paul said unto Barnabas, Let us go again and visit our brethren in every city where we have preached the word of the Lord, and see how they do (Acts 15:36).

Chapter Two

Covenant People Do Not Wait for a Call When There Is a Cause

In First Samuel 17, David arrives on the scene of conflict only to hear the foul language of an uncircumcised Philistine spewing out accusations against the Lord God of Israel. David's times of worship back on the moonlit hillsides as he kept the sheep have made him exceptionally sensitive to ugly words spoken against the Lover of his soul. He is confused as to why no one will silence the rage of this beastly creature.

It seems everyone has an excuse. Their words are grievous to Jesse's youngest son. "Well, it is just not my calling. I have not been called to kill giants." A holy fire begins to kindle in David much like the one he felt when a bear stole one of his father's sheep. He cries out with passion, "*...Is there not a cause?*" (1 Sam. 17:29)

❦ ⟶ ❦

David understood that people of covenant do not have to wait for a call whenever there is a corporate cause. He had learned from his time with the sheep that his individual gifting and calling were never more important than the corporate cause. Giants are devouring our corporate destiny while we wait on some call before we respond to the masses that must have answers.

The Hebrew root of the name *Goliath* means "to denude or to shame, reveal, expose and to exile." The name *David* means "beloved, lover or love token."[1] Even the names of these two key players speak of two diverse models of relationships. One seeks to expose and ultimately exile and excommunicate fallen or hurting people. The other is a man of covenant who covers all who are in need as a token of God's love.

David went from one soldier to another, pleading carefully, "*Is there not a cause?*" Yet, each one seemed to be preoccupied with his own agenda. David sensed that he was not just there to deliver snacks to his brothers. Perhaps that was the moment for which he was born. No one seemed to care that this giant, by denuding the people of God, was bringing reproach against the God of Israel. Again David pleaded, "*Is there not a cause?*"

His brothers mocked him. Others called him names. Some even questioned his motives. David was not detoured or distracted. Someone must stop this loudmouthed giant. As King Saul challenged his credentials and warned him to leave the giant alone, every fiber of David's being continued to scream, "*Is there not a cause?*"

Likewise, God again in quiet patience is raising up Davidic leaders who refuse to wait for a call when there is a cause. How many lives have been ruined as others have sat idly by and watched their injustices, saying, "That is just not my calling"? David understood that you do not have to be called to do what is right.

He hath showed thee, O man, what is good; and what doth the Lord require of thee, but to do justly, and to love mercy, and to walk humbly with thy God? (Micah 6:8)

The cause is greater than the call. If you only move on a call, you may miss the command. Two-thirds of "God" is Go! Moving to the other side of His name, two-thirds of "God" is Do! Go and Do! You don't have to have a call for that. You have a cause. *"Is there not a cause?"*

Covenant people never wait to be told to do what is already expected of them. Covenant people never have to be reminded to be faithful—covenant people *are* faithful.

David's passion was to involve himself where others did not see the need. This man who epitomized covenant could not bear to watch while someone else was being denuded, ashamed, and sent into exile. David knew all too well that these kinds of giants must be put to death.

When Saul became convinced that he could not stop David from trying, he said, "At least let me offer you my covering." With confidence and without hesitation, David rejected the old system of Saul. If what Saul had could work, then why was the giant still alive?

Yesterday's anointing and methods will not silence the giant-sized mountains we face today. It will require more than skill or talent. It will call for more than a handbook on antiquated warfare. We need more than a theory. We are all staring down some real giants. Is the cause burning in your spirit? Do you desire covenant with every cell in your body?

The very thing that Saul and Eliab thought that disqualified David as a possible giant-killer was about to be the thing that God used to vindicate David, Israel, and Israel's God. Real covenant love will slay every shameful and embarrassing Goliath that lifts its ugly head.

The cause was flowing in David's veins and breathing through his nostrils. The more God's man listened to this giant, the more he sounded like a lion. The more he looked at this giant, the more he looked like a bear. David went back in his mind to those days with the sheep on the hill. *"Is there not a cause?"*

For me, the cause is unbreakable covenant relationships that model the Kingdom of God in the earth. The giant Goliath represents any force that tries to hinder that cause. For you, the cause may be different, and the giant may look different, but the strategy is still the same. Goliath must die!

❀ ⟨━━━⟩ ❀

The young sheep-keeper is about to teach the polished big boys a lesson they will not soon forget. God is a covenant-keeper. David has learned some secrets in the field that his brethren have yet to learn.

> *The secret of the Lord is with them that fear Him; and He will show them His covenant* (Psalm 25:14).

God is searching the earth for a new breed of people. This army will not have to be called to action. They will be motivated by covenant love and moved by the cause. They have already endured the ridicule of their siblings and have chosen to reject the armor of Saul. The only question left to answer for them is, *"Is there not a cause?"*

This is not the end of our story. What will David use to defeat the giant? Will the rest of Israel support his quest? What will Saul think? How will his brothers respond? What if the giant wins? David does not have time for those questions now. He is a covenant man. He has found a cause worth dying for. There is a cause. What is this cause? The Truth.

Endnote

1. James Strong, *Strong's Exhaustive Concordance of the Bible* (Peabody, MA; Hendrickson Publishers, n.d.). Goliath—**galah**, #1540; David—**dode** #1730.

Old Testament Covenant Scriptures

David Did Not Wait for a Call When There Was a Cause

And David said, What have I now done? Is there not a cause?

And he turned from him toward another, and spake after the same manner: and the people answered him again after the former manner.

And when the words were heard which David spake, they rehearsed them before Saul: and he sent for him.

And David said to Saul, Let no man's heart fail because of him; thy servant will go and fight with this Philistine (1 Samuel 17:29-32).

Covenant Love Will Conquer Every Enemy

And Saul said to David, Thou art not able to go against this Philistine to fight with him: for thou art but a youth, and he a man of war from his youth.

And David said unto Saul, Thy servant kept his father's sheep, and there came a lion, and a bear, and took a lamb out of the flock:

And I went out after him, and smote him, and delivered it out of his mouth: and when he arose against me, I caught him by his beard, and smote him, and slew him.

Thy servant slew both the lion and the bear: and this uncircumcised Philistine shall be as one of them, seeing he hath defied the armies of the living God.

David said moreover, The Lord that delivered me out of the paw of the lion, and out of the paw of the bear, He will deliver me out of the hand of this Philistine. And Saul said unto David, Go, and the Lord be with thee (1 Samuel 17:33-37).

New Testament Applications

Jesus Demonstrated the Cause
Was Greater Than the Call

Jesus left a revival in Judaea for one Samaritan woman.

He left Judaea, and departed again into Galilee. And He must needs go through Samaria (John 4:3-4).

Paul Did Not Wait for a Call When There Was a Cause

Do all things without murmurings and disputings (Philippians 2:14)

Chapter Three

Covenant People Draw From a Shepherd's Bag

As the crowd watches with amazement, David removes and returns each piece of Saul's armor. Many have ambitiously dreamed of wearing this special uniform. David is not interested in impressing the multitude. He has found the reason for which he has been sent. Covenant purpose is beating in his heart like the sound of a drum. He is not a soldier—he is a servant.

David has no past history of war upon which to lean. But he does have his staff. For many watchful nights, he has carved into that staff the markings of special events and certain victories. What he lacks in history he makes up for with his story. Each of us today needs a fresh understanding of history's significance. Until the importance of history grips your heart, get a grip on His story.

David takes his staff in hand. Energized memories begin to flood his heart. He remembers fighting with lions and bears, but he also remembers victory songs, the Song of the Lord. These songs have flowed out of David's heart and mouth during his darkest nights. Armed with such fresh inspiration, he knows what it will take to defeat the Philistine champion.

All eyes are on David as he turns to face Saul. He gently hands back the armor of manmade steel. Boldly and unashamedly, he begins to speak, "I cannot go with these; for I have not proved them..." (1 Sam. 17:39b).

Saul tries to reason with David, but to no avail. The young shepherd clings to his staff as he chooses five smooth stones from the brook. These smooth stones picture the process of the washing of the water of the Word that removes our rough edges and matures our lives. Once he has chosen the five smooth stones, he places them in "a shepherd's bag" (see 1 Sam. 17:40). With the confused looks from Saul's soldiers at his back, David sets out to face the giant. Goliath stands defiantly in front of him, laughing. His brothers and Saul stand cowardly behind him, laughing. But David knows that covenant love will never fail.

David is drawing from a secret weapon. He is a man of covenant, a man under authority. He has been a shepherd, but he has also met the Chief Shepherd (see 1 Pet. 5:4). *He is drawing from a shepherd's bag.*

❀ ⌐✑✐✒ ❀

The crowds today are seeking the approval of a religious system that validates ministry based upon style instead of substance. Yet God has some reserved shepherds who are not comfortable with the spotlight. The Lord's chosen ones have spent their hours on the back side of the valley building relationships under the moonlight. Instead of packaging themselves for stardom, they have been singing praises under the stars of an open heaven.

Make no mistake; they will shine, but not from fleshly effort. They will glow and flow from service driven from a heart of covenant love. Every person needs a shepherd. Every shepherd needs a shepherd. Without being connected to a shepherd, we have nothing to draw from. *David was drawing from a shepherd's bag.*

As Goliath roared his insults,

> *...David hasted, and ran toward the army to meet the Philistine. And David put his hand in his [shepherd's] bag, and took thence a stone, and slang it, and smote the Philistine in his forehead, that the stone sunk into his forehead; and he fell upon his face to the earth* (1 Samuel 17:48-49).

The key to victory is to consistently draw from the shepherd's bag. You cannot draw from a shepherd's bag without a shepherd. Those who want Kingdom benefits without being properly submitted and related to genuine spiritual eldership and oversight challenge covenant.

In the heat of battle, David was not drawing from a prophet's bag or an evangelist's bag. He was drawing from a shepherd's bag. The shepherd's bag represents the local church and a godly pastor. The five smooth stones correspond to the fivefold ascension-gift ministries (see Eph. 4:11). The reason David was so successful was that he understood what few today understand—the fivefold ministry is only as effective as it is gathered in and under the local church.

No one should have the right to speak a word of greater authority to topple your gigantic circumstances than your shepherd. David rejected the popular, camera-ready leader that was offered in Saul. He chose rather the experience of a humble shepherd servant.

The stone that killed the giant could be the revelation of the corporate Christ that your shepherd has been teaching you (see 1 Cor. 10:4). Let that sink into your forehead. It may be that the biggest giant of all is not outside of us. Goliath could be located between our ears, just above our eyes.

Perhaps the reason so many contemporary preachers keep encouraging us to wear their old armor is because they still are not aware that the "the weapons of our warfare are not carnal" (2 Cor. 10:4a). The giant we fear is not a computer chip or enemy submarine missiles. The giant sized obstacles we must deal with are covenant-breaking Christians who will not submit to a local shepherd. They go from conference to conference, ever looking for a new stone to throw at their problem. The stone needs to sink deep into our own forehead first.

> *Change your mind and attitude, or else I will come to you suddenly and fight against them with the sword of My mouth. Let everyone who can hear, listen to what the Spirit is saying to the churches: Everyone who is victorious shall eat of the hidden manna, the secret nourishment from heaven; and I will give to each a white stone, and on the stone will be engraved a new name that no one else knows except the one receiving it* (Revelation 2:16-17 TLB).

We need to change the way we think. Support godly extralocal ministries that strengthen the local church, but never forget there is no substitute for the local shepherd. *David drew from a shepherd's bag.*

The Philistine army watched in shock as their champion fell to the ground. Saul's army stood in disbelief as the Philistine army fled in horror. The men of Israel and Judah then arose, shouted, and pursued after the army of the Philistines. David had won the battle without a sword. He was still a shepherd, and *he was still drawing from a shepherd's bag.*

As David decapitated Goliath, he was beheading other giants as well. Attitudes were changing. He was no longer just the youngest and a keeper of the sheep. He was now Israel's deliverer. He had won the day.

To every shepherd who has remained faithful, don't faint now. Don't sell out to Saul! The Day of the Lord has dawned. The showdown is coming. God will again reject man's glitter and glamour, anointing *those that draw from a shepherd's bag.*

Choices made at this critical time in history will determine what God is able to do through us. Stay connected to the shepherds God has placed over you. The greatest attack will be leveled against covenant, and it will be aimed at real shepherds. Do not abandon them when they need you most. They did not abandon you in your time of greatest need.

❀ ⋯⋯ ❀

Now all of Israel is aware of what David knew all along. If you are in covenant and *draw from a shepherd's bag*, then giants really do die.

David's covenant journey has begun. Yet he appears to be a man of covenant without anyone to keep covenant with. Covenant is not covenant if we remain alone. Man was not created to be alone. "And the Lord God said, It is not good that the man should be alone..." (Gen. 2:18).

God created a help-meet for man. Through the woman, he provided a level of covenant that would be a pattern of the relationship that would exist between Jesus and the Church. "This is a great mystery: but I speak concerning Christ and the church" (Eph. 5:32).

There is another kind of covenantal level that God is establishing today. It is covenant between people that He knits and joins together for His own purposes. This covenant is just as real and powerful as the covenant of marriage. It simply operates in a different dimension.

David has fed the sheep, served the king, been faithful over his father's flock, and confronted and killed Goliath. He has accomplished all these things with covenant beating in his heart. It has not been in vain, because somewhere there is someone as deeply committed to covenant as he is. When he finds him, his life will be changed forever. Perhaps that someone is not that far away.

Old Testament Covenant Scriptures

David Drew From the Shepherd's Bag

And he took his staff in his hand, and chose him five smooth stones out of the brook, and put them in a shepherd's bag which he had, even in a scrip; and his sling was in his hand: and he drew near to the Philistine.

And David put his hand in his bag, and took thence a stone, and slang it, and smote the Philistine in his forehead, that the stone sunk into his forehead; and he fell upon his face to the earth (1 Samuel 17:40,49).

Covenant Keeping Ensures Final Victory

So David prevailed over the Philistine with a sling and with a stone, and smote the Philistine, and slew him; but there was no sword in the hand of David (1 Samuel 17:50).

New Testament Applications

Jesus Drew From the Shepherd's Bag

Then answered Jesus and said unto them, Verily, verily, I say unto you, The Son can do nothing of Himself, but what He seeth the Father do: for what things soever He doeth, these also doeth the Son likewise.

I can of Mine own self do nothing: as I hear, I judge: and My judgment is just; because I seek not Mine own will, but the will of the Father which hath sent Me (John 5:19,30).

Then said Jesus unto them, When ye have lifted up the Son of man, then shall ye know that I am He, and that I do nothing of Myself; but as My Father hath taught Me, I speak these things (John 8:28).

Paul Drew From the Shepherd's Bag

For I determined not to know any thing among you, save Jesus Christ, and Him crucified (1 Corinthians 2:2).

But when it pleased God, who separated me from my mother's womb, and called me by His grace, to reveal His Son in me, that I might preach Him among the heathen; immediately I conferred not with flesh and blood (Galatians 1:15-16).

Chapter Four

Covenant People Will Find Someone They Can Lose Themselves In

David is a hero in the eyes of Israel and Judah. Yet in his own heart, David is still just a lonely shepherd. How can so many people be singing his praises while he himself feels so unfulfilled? He has the head of the Philistine champion in his hand, but in his heart, he does not feel like a giant-killer.

Saul, seeing David returning from the slaughter of the Philistine, seeks to benefit from the young lad's sudden popularity. The opportunistic king calls for David and begins to inquire as to who he is and what his future plans are. The intelligent politician that this people's king has become is calculating how he might further his own agenda from a relationship with the newly discovered hero. With a few of his men and his son Jonathan by his side, Saul begins to craftily bait the shepherd boy.

David is not nearly as naïve as Saul is hoping he will be. He has dealt with lions and bears and wolves before. David is not really interested in political relationships. Everything in him desires meaningful covenant relationships that will produce prophetic purpose. David knows in his heart that the killing of Goliath is not the end, but only a means to finding fulfillment to his destiny. Furthermore, the young psalmist has discovered that real fulfillment comes from *losing yourself in someone else*, from finding a cause bigger than yourself to live for.

As David begins to speak, it becomes clear that Saul has underestimated the shepherd's heart. But Jonathan is captivated by David's words. This young prince has lived for years under the control and ambitious dictatorship of his father. He is hungry and ready for real relationship that is not driven by self-service. Jonathan is ready to *lose himself in someone else*.

❈ ⋯⋙⋘⋯ ❈

The question that turned the direction of David's life was the answer that likewise turned Jonathan's heart. "And Saul said to him, Whose son art thou, thou young man? And David answered, I am the son of thy servant Jesse the Bethlehemite" (1 Sam. 17:58). This question steered the destinies of David and Jonathan into a new path.

As David described his father, Jesse, Jonathan knew that the young shepherd had something in his father that the young prince had never experienced. Saul may have produced the natural seed that brought Jonathan into being, but Saul had fallen far short of being a father. Listening to David talk, Jonathan realized it took more than procreation to make a man a father. Jonathan had become desperate to *lose himself in someone else*.

And it came to pass, when he had made an end of speaking unto Saul, that the soul of Jonathan was knit with the soul of

David, and Jonathan loved him as his own soul (1 Samuel 18:1).

Who could have possibly imagined that the covenant brother that David had longed for would come from the house of Saul? Likewise, who could have imagined that a son of Saul would desire and be such a man of covenant?

That day Saul insisted that David stay in the palace and go no more home to his father. Saul's motive was self-serving, but God had a covenant connection in the making. Jonathan and David were about to *lose themselves in each other.*

God again today is connecting people, for His purposes, who are tired of political, controlling relationships that only serve to exalt flesh. He is joining people who are willing to serve each other, willing to *lose themselves in someone else*—people who care more about their covenant brother or sister than they do about themselves.

> *Let nothing be done through strife or vainglory; but in lowliness of mind let each esteem other better than themselves. Look not every man on his own things, but every man also on the things of others* (Philippians 2:3-4).

You may be surprised to whom God fastens you today. Divine connections are not based upon personality, but upon Kingdom purpose and potential. They are not based upon theological convictions. God may join us together with people who were raised in the house of Saul. Some associations will be with people delivered straight out of deep sin. The only issue with God is His own purpose. The only real question is, "Are you willing to lose yourself in someone else?"

The Hebrew word that describes what happened when the soul of Jonathan was "knit" with David is *qashar* and it is used only this one time in the Bible. It means, "to tie, to physically confine or compact together in a league of love; to knit stronger together."

This definition would insinuate covenant by the Spirit is a binding agreement for life. The Spirit, however, only enforces it.

The Scripture says that the "soul" of Jonathan was knit with the soul of David. *Soul* is from the Hebrew word *naphash*, which is the root word of *nephesh*. These definitions, as given by *Strong's Exhaustive Concordance of the Bible* (#5314 and 5315), mean "breath and vitality." In real covenant, God breathes on the relationship between two people, causing the vitality of their individual purposes to become inseparable from one another. We are nothing without someone else. Individualism must die. *We must lose ourselves in someone else.*

> *Then Jonathan and David made a covenant, because he loved him as his own soul* (1 Samuel 18:3).

When the Scripture says that Jonathan "loved" David as his own soul, it is not the same kind of "love" as when Michal is stated to have "loved" David or as when Israel and Judah were said to have "loved" David. This kind of covenant love enables one to prefer his brother above himself. Michal loved David for his accomplishments. Israel and Judah loved the young giant-killer for the victory he had won for them. Jonathan loved David by the Spirit for who he was, not for what he did.

> *And Jonathan stripped himself of the robe that was upon him, and gave it to David, and his garments, even to his sword, and to his bow, and to his girdle* (1 Samuel 18:4).

The phrase "stripped himself" reveals that these two young men were beginning to *lose themselves in each other*. As Jonathan gave David his princely robe of authority, David clothed Jonathan with his humility. They stood face-to-face, naked and unashamed. David was *losing himself in* Jonathan, and Jonathan was *losing himself in* David.

Covenant people have nothing to hide from one another. They are not afraid of seeing the flaws in their brother or sister. When God knits your heart with someone, it goes deeper than feelings. This depth of covenantal commitment can only be understood by experiencing it.

Covenant people have all things in common, but that does not mean that covenant is a common thing. A person cannot continue to sin and walk in covenant. To sin is to walk out of covenant. My covenant brother cannot steal from me because whatever I have is already his. Covenant brothers cannot sin against each other. Sin is living outside of covenant. Righteousness is living inside of covenant.

Jonathan's robe placed him next in line to be king. Yet, David had been anointed in a private ceremony by Prophet Samuel to be the next monarch because God had already rejected Saul. Saul had no idea that God had already picked his replacement, and that the replacement was living in his own house! Jonathan was giving up his right to the throne to David. Yet, when David would reign, Jonathan would reign together with him because they had *lost themselves in each other.*

God is searching the earth for men and women who have had their souls knit together with someone other than themselves. He is looking for men and women who are willing to invest themselves in the successes of others. He seeks for men and women who are not insecure and arrogant. Insecure men and women cannot be covenant people, because insecure people will not lose themselves in another person.

Covenant people are stable and humble enough to place the needs and success of others above their own. You will know you have found your covenant connection when your heart is knit in the covenant way, and you want *to lose yourself in this someone else.* Covenant cannot be self-serving; it is about prophetic purpose. You can recognize when relationships are God-ordained—they will release your destiny. Covenant people are designed to *lose themselves in someone else.* Real fulfillment comes from assisting your covenant connections in finding their destiny and reaching their goals. As with Joshua of old, you will truly *cause others to inherit!*

Old Testament Covenant Scriptures

David Lost Himself in Jonathan

And it came to pass, when he had made an end of speaking unto Saul, that the soul of Jonathan was knit with the soul of David, and Jonathan loved him as his own soul.

Then Jonathan and David made a covenant, because he loved him as his own soul.

And Jonathan stripped himself of the robe that was upon him, and gave it to David, and his garments, even to his sword, and to his bow, and to his girdle (1 Samuel 18:1,3-4).

New Testament Applications

Jesus Lost Himself in Others

I am the good shepherd: the good shepherd giveth His life for the sheep (John 10:11).

He that findeth his life shall lose it: and he that loseth his life for My sake shall find it (Matthew 10:39).

And if ye have not been faithful in that which is another man's, who shall give you that which is your own? (Luke 16:12)

Paul Lost Himself in Timothy and Others

Unto Timothy, my own son in the faith: Grace, mercy, and peace, from God our Father and Jesus Christ our Lord (1 Timothy 1:2).

And I will very gladly spend and be spent for you; though the more abundantly I love you, the less I be loved (2 Corinthians 12:15).

Chapter Five

Covenant People Behave Themselves Wisely

Political posturing did not work then, nor will it survive today. Saul has supposed that David's living in his home will certainly enhance his own donations and increase his own popularity. What he does not know is that you cannot fake covenant. You may know a covenant man or woman, but that does not make *you* a covenant man or woman.

Jonathan has become united with the purpose of God in David's life and ministry. David has become accepted in the sight of all the men of war and all the people, not to mention Saul's own servants. He has done so by *behaving himself wisely*.

❊ ⚊⚊⚊⚊ ❊

To further his own agenda, Saul set David over the armies of war. The man of covenant thereby understood that he must represent Saul and not himself. So David went out wherever Saul sent him. David was always *sent* to his mission. He never just struck out on his own. Covenant people are commissioned. They operate under command.

As careful as David was to never draw attention to himself, it seemed the people always venerated him. Covenant people will be celebrated because they always put others first. The world is looking for covenant people who are not selfish. Covenant people seek to do what is best for others even at their own expense.

Covenant people are not jealous of others who succeed. Saul had no concept of covenant. He was a jealous, self-serving, religious tyrant. Religion always seeks to promote itself. Covenant always promotes the Lord and others.

The battle began then as it often does today, because of jealousy. There was a parade for Saul to celebrate the victory over the Philistine champion. This occasion was to honor Saul. But the women paraded into the streets singing and dancing, together exclaiming, "Saul hath slain his thousands, and David his ten thousands" (1 Sam. 18:7b). The insecurity and jealousy in Saul could not take any compliments going to anyone but himself.

And Saul was very wroth, and the saying displeased him; and he said, They have ascribed unto David ten thousands, and to me they have ascribed but thousands: and what can he have more but the kingdom? And Saul eyed David from that day and forward (1 Samuel 18:8-9).

Insecurity, suspicion, and jealousy are the three biggest threats to covenant. Saul was baptized in all three. He was insecure because the Lord was with David and was departed from him (see 1 Sam. 18:12). He was suspicious of David because the people loved David. Saul had wrong motives, so he assumed David also had bad intentions. He was jealous because of the attention David was getting from Jonathan, all the people, and even his own servants. Yet, David continued *to behave himself wisely.*

Religious systems and denominations will bring you into their arena and treat you like royalty, but they refuse to change. The status quo is all that is accepted. Religion is political, not prophetic. It looks for hirelings, not covenant servants. Covenant people are a threat to religious systems because covenant people are real about their relationships. Religious people only build relationships for their own temporary purposes, only later to discard them.

Saul became obsessed with destroying David, but in the process destroyed himself. To every covenant-breaker, I issue this warning: Your insecurity, suspicion, and jealousy are going to cause you to self-destruct. Grow up, heal, trust, and support others.

In an hour when men are infatuated with titles and position, God is looking for men and women who will *behave themselves wisely*. David continued to serve Saul faithfully. David was not in the king's palace for public recognition and acclamation. His heart was now joined to the son of Saul. Nothing was worth losing this covenant relationship. He must *behave himself wisely*.

Titles and position are not of themselves wrong; in fact, they are needed and necessary. The problem is the way people jockey for titles and position instead of allowing God to bestow these honors and promotions. Titles are simply job descriptions, and positions are simply those spheres in which you fulfill that description. David never sought either, yet both came to him because *he behaved himself wisely*.

No matter how Saul mistreated David, the young shepherd never ceased to *behave himself wisely*. Saul even twice sought to kill David with a javelin. David escaped out of his hand both times, yet he never allowed bitterness to take root in his spirit.

Saul even prohesied as he threw the javelin at David (see 1 Sam. 18:10-11). Religious systems will prophesy over you as they seek to kill you. The ability for an individual or an organization to prophesy accurately does not necessarily indicate confirmation of God's approval upon that individual or group. God is not nearly as impressed with gifts as He is with fruit. Gifts can be taught, but fruit must be developed. Character cannot be imparted through the laying on of hands. It must be built or grown. Keen human observation often masquerades as so-called prophetic gifting. Fruit, the character and nature of Christ, cannot be faked or counterfeited. Saul might have been able to prophesy, but David's covenant heart kept him faithful. Saul had a gift, but David had fruit. That's why God had rejected Saul and had chosen David.

Saul, in an effort to keep David under surveillance, offered to give him Merab, his oldest daughter, to wife. David *behaved himself wisely* and said, "I am not worthy to be the son-in-law of the king" (see 1 Sam. 18:18). Saul then sent David to battle, hoping that he might be killed. While David was away, Saul gave Merab to Adriel as a wife. David returned to witness Saul's deceit, yet still *behaved himself wisely.*

Merab by definition means "increase."[1] Saul was offering to increase David so long as his old order could remain in control. Political relationships are always about control. Religious leaders will prophesy your increase so long as you stay under their thumb. Consider yourself warned—they have no intention of giving you increase. It is just a ploy to get you to go to battle for them. *Adriel* means "arrangement within the flock."[2] While David was away at battle, Saul gave "increase" to an "arrangement within the flock." Do not be deceived. People who do not understand covenant will not keep their word. They will only support their own flock.

David survived the battle and returned home to brutally discover that his increase had been given to someone else. If this story sounds familiar, you may be surrounded by covenant-breakers. Learn from David. Do not join them by breaking covenant. Remain faithful and then watch God prove Himself on your behalf. Be like David, and *behave yourself wisely.*

Saul had another daughter who had fallen for David. David again used the line, "I am not worthy to be the son-in-law of the king" (see 1 Sam. 18:23). Saul made an agreement with David that he would give Michal to wife in exchange for one hundred Philistine foreskins. Once more, Saul again expected David to be killed by the enemy (see 1 Sam. 18:25).

Yet David exceeded Saul's request. He killed 200 Philistines and brought their foreskins to Saul. Saul gave Michal to David to be his wife. Saul then realized that the Lord was with David, and that both Michal and Jonathan loved David. All the servants of Saul were then hailing David's name. Everywhere that Saul turned, David was being praised. His insane jealousy escalated.

And Saul was yet the more afraid of David; and Saul became David's enemy continually (1 Samuel 18:29).

❈ ⌗⌗⌗⌗⌗ ❈

The more Saul uses and abuses David, the more God's covenant man submits and remains faithful. He has been given Michal when he was promised Merab. *Michal* means "rivulet, a small stream or brook."[3] He has been promised great increase, but he has to settle for a small brook. Covenant people will be patient with little, even when they have been promised much.

David is fully aware that God is about to change the whole order of things. He has a true covenant brother in Jonathan. What more could he want? So, for now, he chooses to continue *to behave himself wisely.*

Saul may despise him, but Jonathan loves David for who he is. Michal loves David for what he has accomplished. Israel and Judah love David for what he has done for them. God loves David because he has a wise covenant heart. *Covenant people behave themselves wisely.*

Endnotes

1. James Strong, *Strong's Exhaustive Concordance of the Bible* (Peabody, MA: Hendrickson Publishers, n.d.), **merab**, #4764

2. *Strong's*, **Adriyel**, #5741. Also see **eder**, #5739—"arrangement of or within the flock."

3. *Strong's*, **Miykal**, #4324.

Old Testament Covenant Scriptures

David Behaved Wisely

And David went out whithersoever Saul sent him, and behaved himself wisely: and Saul set him over the men of war, and he was accepted in the sight of all the people, and also in the sight of Saul's servants.

And David behaved himself wisely in all his ways; and the Lord was with him (1 Samuel 18:5,14).

When Covenant People Behave Wisely, Others Take Notice

Wherefore when Saul saw that [David] behaved himself very wisely, he was afraid of him.

Then the princes of the Philistines went forth: and it came to pass, after they went forth, that David behaved himself more wisely than all the servants of Saul; so that his name was much set by (1 Samuel 18:15,30).

New Testament Applications

Jesus Behaved Wisely

The baptism of John, whence was it? from heaven, or of men? And they reasoned with themselves, saying, If we shall say, From heaven; He will say unto us, Why did ye not then believe him?

But if we shall say, Of men; we fear the people; for all hold John as a prophet.

And they answered Jesus, and said, We cannot tell. And He said unto them, Neither tell I you by what authority I do these things (Matthew 21:25-27).

Behold, I send you forth as sheep in the midst of wolves: be ye therefore wise as serpents, and harmless as doves (Matthew 10:16).

Paul Behaved Wisely

To the weak became I as weak, that I might gain the weak: I am made all things to all men, that I might by all means save some (1 Corinthians 9:22).

For yourselves know how ye ought to follow us: for we behaved not ourselves disorderly among you (2 Thessalonians 3:7).

Chapter Six

Covenant People Delight in and Serve Each Other

Jealousy, insecurity, and suspicion have fueled Saul's anger and rage. He has become a man out of control, sensing that the day approaches in which he will be replaced. The Lord has departed from him. Two of his own children have become loyal to David. His whole kingdom views David as a hero. This cannot be! This young ruddy shepherd boy has captured the hearts of an entire nation. Suddenly, Saul realizes that his successor, until recently, had been living in his own house! It is not to be his own son, but this shepherd-boy turned soldier.

He plots to destroy David, but every scheme backfires. There must be a way to trick this covenant man into betrayal, or at least to behave himself unwisely. He must have a weakness. Does God really cover covenant people even in their weaknesses? The insecure king cannot take it anymore.

Saul calls an emergency board meeting with Prince Jonathan and all the servants. Surely his own son has enough of Saul's blood that he has ambitions to be the next king. Saul plays his final hand. If David is not stopped, Jonathan will never be king. David must be killed.

What Saul has never understood is the covenant that was cut between David and Jonathan. Jonathan has already relinquished to David his right to the throne. Jonathan is a covenant man who has lost himself in David. Jonathan *delights much in* David. Jonathan only wants *to serve* David the way David has served Saul.

❀ ⌁⌁⌁ ❀

The young prince tried to reason with his father. The more he tried to persuade Saul, the angrier Saul became. After all, orders had been given to "kill David" (see 1 Sam. 19:1).

Jonathan had a covenant with David that went deeper than the blood that was flowing through his veins. The blood of the lamb that they had used in their ceremonial covenant was thicker than the blood he had inherited from his natural father. The lamb was a servant. The Messianic Lamb, the greatest Son of David, was later led to the slaughter without opening His mouth (see Mt. 1:1; Acts 8:32). Jonathan was one with the purpose of God in David. He was a servant.

Jonathan characterized the sons of God who are "born, not of blood, nor of the will of the flesh, nor of the will of man, but of God" (Jn. 1:13).

Jonathan *delighted much in* David and was committed *to serve* him. No one or nothing was going to break this covenant. He felt certain that in time he could change Saul's mind about David. After all, David had never wanted the throne. He had always been submissive, always doing what was best for everyone else.

Jonathan instructed David to take heed to himself at least until morning. Jonathan would talk to Saul and reason with him. Surely Saul would come to his senses. These two boys *delighted in and served each other.* They had waited forever to find each other. Jealousy and insecurity could not break up their foreordained union.

> *But Jonathan Saul's son delighted much in David: and Jonathan told David, saying, Saul my father seeketh to kill thee: now therefore, I pray thee, take heed to thyself until the morning, and abide in a secret place, and hide thyself* (1 Samuel 19:2).

For every covenant person who has been faithful, only to be attacked, take heed to the words in the preceding verse. Religion will seek to kill you. If not physically, it will seek to destroy you and your covenant with slander, seduction, and rumors. But know this: There is a place for you to hide until the morning.

I meet men and women weekly who have been devastated by people leaving their families, churches, jobs, and relationships. These people who break relationships seek to destroy the folks they leave behind. Sadly, these cowards are often the ones who covenant people have invested the most time and energy into. Sometimes those whom covenant people *delighted in and served* are the ones who desert with the nastiest attitude. David had poured his whole life into Saul and gotten nothing but heartache. Nothing, that is, but his covenant with Jonathan. His covenant with Jonathan was worth the pain of Saul.

The morning will come. Right now it may seem that the night will last forever, but take heed to thyself—the morning will come! Remember that you are a person of covenant. Abiding is a part of your nature. All covenant people are familiar with a secret place that is only shared in covenant. Stay there until morning. Hide yourself in the covenant promise you have with God.

> *He that dwelleth in the secret place of the most High shall abide under the shadow of the Almighty* (Psalm 91:1).

Jonathan intervened on David's behalf, pointing out David's innocence. Surely Israel would not support the killing of innocent blood. "And Saul hearkened unto the voice of Jonathan: and Saul sware, As the Lord liveth, he shall not be slain" (1 Sam. 19:6).

Things seemed to be back to normal. David was serving in Saul's army and court. Jonathan and David were meeting in secret places *delighting in and serving each other*. Michal and David seemed to be at harmony even though at times she behaved a lot like her daddy. Be careful, friend. Things never remain normal with people that do not understand covenant.

Saul's rage returned. While David played on his harp, Saul again threw the javelin at David, who desperately escaped into the night. Religion can hide for a season in the midst of covenant but the enemy will eventually resurface.

Michal warned David that her father would not stop until David was murdered. She sent him into the night to Prophet Samuel at Naioth in Ramah. *Naioth* comes from a Hebrew root that means "rest."[1] *Ramah* means "high place."[2] In those night seasons when men seek to destroy your life, rejoice to know that you have a high priest that has secured your high place of rest.

It was then clear to David that there was but a step between himself and death. Samuel reassured David that God had a plan for his life and that he could not die until he finished his purpose. The prophet reminded him of the consecration service at Jesse's house. God had already rejected Saul at that time. Samuel told David he must not hinder what God had ordained.

I want to affirm every covenant man and woman. However it looks right now, God has a plan for your life. You cannot die until you finish your purpose. God chose you long before now, and you cannot stop the process. You are destined to rule and reign.

David stole away to spend time with Jonathan and to warn him that there would be no stopping Saul. Jonathan had a tough time believing that his father would break his word, but Saul had never understood covenant. While Jonathan and David met, Saul was lying naked in front of Samuel prophesying (see 1 Sam. 19:24).

Covenant-breakers may be open and bare for a moment when the Spirit of God is upon them, but underneath their prophetic cloak is a spirit of division and murder. Saul among the prophets behaved like the prophets, but away from them he was a raving, self-centered madman. Again, gifting is not God's seal of approval.

❋ ⚬⚬⚬⚬⚬⚬ ❋

Jonathan is now forced to decide between his natural father and his covenant brother. There really is no choice. Covenant is deeper and thicker than blood. He is not born of blood; he is born of the will of God.

Covenant is not always easy. It will come with a high price tag. Jesus said, "Who is My mother? and who are My brethren? And He stretched forth His hand toward His disciples, and said, Behold My mother and My brethren! For whosoever shall do the will of My Father which is in heaven, the same is My brother, and sister, and mother (Mt. 12:48b-50).

The decision has been made. The covenant is in place. *They delight in and serve each other.* Jonathan says unto David, "Whatsoever thy soul desireth, I will even do it for thee" (1 Sam. 20:4).

Endnotes

1. James Strong, *Strong's Exhasustive Concordance of the Bible* (Peabody, MA: Hendrickson Publishers, n.d.), **navah**, #5115.

2. *Strong's*, **râmâh**, #7413.

Old Testament Covenant Scriptures

Covenant Is Deeper and Thicker Than Blood

But Jonathan Saul's son delighted much in David: and Jonathan told David, saying, Saul my father seeketh to kill thee: now therefore, I pray thee, take heed to thyself until the morning, and abide in a secret place, and hide thyself (1 Samuel 19:2).

Then said Jonathan unto David, Whatsoever thy soul desireth, I will even do it for thee.

So Jonathan made a covenant with the house of David, saying, Let the Lord even require it at the hand of David's enemies.

And Jonathan caused David to swear again, because he loved him: for he loved him as he loved his own soul (1 Samuel 20:4,16,17).

New Testament Applications

Jesus Was a Servant

And whosoever will be chief among you, let him be your servant: even as the Son of man came not to be ministered unto, but to minister, and to give His life a ransom for many (Matthew 20:27-28).

Paul Was a Servant

For we preach not ourselves, but Christ Jesus the Lord; and ourselves your servants for Jesus' sake (2 Corinthians 4:5).

Chapter Seven

Covenant People Are Intimate and Passionate

There is nothing perverted or unnatural about David and Jonathan's relationship. That which has happened between them is supernatural. God has knitted their souls together because of greater Kingdom purpose. God joins people together in levels of intimacy and passion that religious and lost people cannot understand. This is not unnatural affection. This is supernatural connection. It is all about purpose, not flesh.

Western civilization's thinking has programmed us that passion and intimacy can only be achieved in a sensual, physical way. That is precisely why Americans seldom fulfill relationships with friends and colleagues. We do not think that it is possible. Yet God has ordained that every man has a man who will be a covenant brother to him. Every woman is to have a woman who will be a covenant sister to her. This can only be wrought through the Holy Spirit connecting us with the right brother or sister.

Covenant people are intimate and passionate. These words are not about physical fulfillment, but spiritual fulfillment and purpose. It has been stated accurately that worship is the passion of God. We reveal our passion to God three ways: our worship of Him, our service to Him, and our relationship with each other. Jesus said, "Inasmuch as ye have done it unto one of the least of these My brethren, ye have done it unto Me" (Mt. 25:40).

Jonathan and David are inseparable because of greater purpose. They are *passionate* and *intimate* with each other because God has caused them to be fulfilled in each other. Their relationship does not take away from their relationships with other people. What makes them different toward each other is God's divine knitting.

❀ ⟡ ❀

Covenant relationships are not about friendships. Being a friend does not necessarily mean you have covenant. You pick your own friends, but God establishes your covenants by His own choosings. Friendships can come and go. Covenants are for life.

David was married to Michal, the sister of Jonathan, and the daughter of Saul. He was a faithful servant of Saul. Servants and soldiers who admired him surrounded him. He had many friends, but his being knit to Jonathan was about a shared purpose.

David had a marriage covenant that was real and honorable. He was submitted under Saul and had soldiers and servants under him, and these were real and honorable covenants. Yet, he needed a peer-level covenant, and that was what he had found in Jonathan.

The New Webster's Dictionary defines *passion* as "a compelling emotion or devotion." David and Jonathan were compelled to be devoted to each other even when they had to choose between natural relationships. Spiritual relationships must always take precedence. *Covenant people are passionate*.

Webster's likewise defines *intimate* to mean "private; personal and familiar with." What these two men of covenant shared was private and personal; they were exceptionally familiar with each other. Everyone needs someone that they can share their private and personal matters with—someone who is familiar with their purpose and destiny. Don't try to pick and choose this person. Let God connect you. *Covenant people are intimate.*

Since the day they had made a covenant between themselves, Jonathan and David never hid a thing from each other. They had started their relationship by being bare in each other's sight and by exchanging garments. It was then revealed to Jonathan that Saul was going to kill David. David was waiting in a secret place in the field for word from Jonathan. Jonathan knew he could not hide this news from David. But if he told him, they might never see each other again. Saul's son was filled with grief and anguish.

The look on Jonathan's face confirmed what David already knew in his heart. Both began to cry as they embraced and greeted each other with a "holy kiss" (see Rom. 16:16; 1 Thess. 5:26). In their hearts, this kiss felt like a kiss of betrayal, yet both knew their commitment to each other was secure. Their hearts were so full of pain and emotion that they fell to the ground. As they lay there on the ground crying and holding each other, David wondered out loud, "Why does Saul hate me so?" Jonathan tried to encourage David, but he needed encouragement himself. When they could cry no more, they strengthened their covenant once more (see 1 Sam. 20:41-42).

> *At last Jonathan said to David, "Cheer up, for we have entrusted each other and each other's children into God's hands forever." So they parted, David going away and Jonathan returning to the city* (1 Samuel 20:42 TLB).

As they walked away from each other that day, they knew this moment was not to be a good-bye forever. The pain felt like it would never end. They remembered the intimate details of their life and covenant, the passion they had felt and shared concerning God's purpose for their lives. Saul could not disannul their covenant. It was filled with too many *intimate and passionate* memories. What they felt was not uncommon for covenant people.

Covenant-breakers have always been jealous of covenant-keepers, ever seeking to destroy those godly relationships. Saul would continue to try to tear down David and keep him separated from Jonathan, but God had established their covenant bond. Nothing could destroy this covenant, not even death. It took the death of a lamb to start this covenant, so the death of a person could not nullify it. *Intimate and passionate* relationship would win out in the end.

David would eventually say of Jonathan's death, "I am distressed for thee, my brother Jonathan: very pleasant hast thou been unto me: thy love to me was wonderful, passing the love of women" (2 Sam. 1:26).

Do not allow the thinking of western civilization or contemporary Christendom to rob you of real covenant relationships. Hedonistic, western thought is that if something no longer feels good, get rid of it. Accordingly, it is easy to discard marriage, jobs, your church, and your covenant relationships. God the Father transcends the western world and the platforms of modern high-tech Christianity.

Each of us is predestined to connect with a covenant brother or sister. In Revelation 1:9, John refers to himself as our "brother, and companion in tribulation." These two words, *brother* and *companion*, perfectly describe David and Jonathan's *relationship*.

The word *brother* used in Revelation chapter one comes from the Greek word *adelphos*, which means "womb brother."[1] It is derived from the Greek word *Alpha*. John is saying, "I am your womb brother from the beginning, from the womb of the morning" (compare Ps. 110:3). Covenant connections are our womb brothers and sisters. We have been conceived for the same purpose from the same womb. The phrase "from the beginning" tells us that these relationships were preordained from the foundation of the world.

The word *companion* adds another dimension to the equation.[2] It means "partaker or joined with; literally, to be connected at the hip." Not only are we born for the same purpose and from the same womb, but we also are connected at the hipbone.

Brother reveals the family connection that provides the passionate portion of the relationship. *Companion* sets forth the supernatural connection that provides the intimate portion of the relationship. *Covenant people are intimate and passionate.*

※ ～～～～ ※

David and Jonathan have discovered this kind of covenant in each other. Their companionship is expressed in the time of their tribulation. "A friend loveth at all times, and a brother is born for adversity" (Prov. 17:17).

Real relationships survive the test of tribulation and pressure. This kind of covenant is of God. Everyone needs a covenant relationship that is *intimate and passionate.* David and Jonathan are womb brothers, companions in tribulation.

Are you connected to anyone at the hipbone? Have you found your covenant womb brother or sister? If not, just wait. Your desire will create your opportunity. Don't try to pick them by yourself. Wait on God to bring them to you, to knit you to them. He will bless your life as you learn to experience a new level of *intimate and passionate covenant.*

Endnotes

1. James Strong, *Strong's Exhaustive Concordance of the Bible* (Peabody, MA: Hendrickson Publishing, n.d.), **adelphos**, #80.

2. *Strong's*, #4791/4862/2844.

Old Testament Covenant Scriptures

Covenant Forges New Spiritual Loyalties

And Jonathan caused David to swear again, because he loved him: for he loved him as he loved his own soul.

Then Saul's anger was kindled against Jonathan, and he said unto him, Thou son of the perverse rebellious woman, do not I know that thou hast chosen the son of Jesse to thine own confusion, and unto the confusion of thy mother's nakedness?

And Saul cast a javelin at him to smite him: whereby Jonathan knew that it was determined of his father to slay David.

And as soon as the lad was gone, David arose out of a place toward the south, and fell on his face to the ground, and bowed himself three times: and they kissed one another, and wept one with another, until David exceeded.

And Jonathan said to David, Go in peace, forasmuch as we have sworn both of us in the name of the Lord, saying, The Lord be between me and thee, and between my seed and thy seed for ever. And he arose and departed: and Jonathan went into the city (1 Samuel 20:17,30,33,41,42).

New Testament Applications

Jesus Is Intimate and Passionate

Jesus answered and said unto him, If a man love Me, he will keep My words: and My Father will love him, and We will come unto him, and make Our abode with him (John 14:23).

Behold, I stand at the door, and knock: if any man hear My voice, and open the door, I will come in to him, and will sup with him, and he with Me (Revelation 3:20).

Paul Was Intimate and Passionate

So being affectionately desirous of you, we were willing to have imparted unto you, not the gospel of God only, but also our own souls, because ye were dear unto us (1 Thesslonians 2:8).

Chapter Eight

Covenant People Will Invest in the Outcast

David has walked away from Jonathan with nothing but memories. He cannot return to take his belongings, for Saul would surely kill him. He seems to be starting all over again, but it wasn't that long ago that he was but a simple sheep-keeper. He has killed lions and bears. He has slain the Philistine champion and tens of thousands of Philistines for Saul. Now, Saul wants to kill him. He doesn't feel like a giant-killer anymore. He doesn't even have a weapon.

Fearing for his life, David runs to Ahimelech the priest for food and hopefully a weapon. When he arrives, there is no food, only the hallowed communion bread (see 1 Sam. 21:1-6). He asks for five loaves of bread and receives communion instead. The five loaves could represent the fivefold ministry (see Eph. 4:11) or the grace that David is about to receive.

Instead of always seeking the aid of the fivefold ministry, we are learning the added blessing of the assistance that comes from communion with God and His saints. The priest reminds him of covenant by giving him communion bread. Communion is a covenant of the Church and should be observed as such (see 1 Cor. 11:23-30).

Though a covenant man, David panics and begins to rely on human strength. He asks for any weapons that might be in the temple. Ahimelech is confused by David's sudden dependence on carnal weapons. Often, when in fear, we go back to comfort zones of the flesh. Surely, this covenant man must know that "the weapons of our warfare are not carnal, but mighty through God to the pulling down of strong holds (2 Cor. 10:4). To remind David of his covenant with God, the priest says, "The sword of Goliath the Philistine, whom thou slewest in the valley of Elah, behold, it is here wrapped in a cloth behind the ephod: if thou wilt take that, take it: for there is no other save that here. And David said, There is none like that; give it me" (1 Sam. 21:9).

Ahimelech points David to the ephod and the sword of Goliath behind it. This prophetic picture shows that our victories have always been behind our priestly garments, not our soldier's uniform. Our greatest weapon is still our priestly ephod of worship and praise. The only weapon David has is the past weapon he has already taken from the Philistine champion. Covenant people must remind themselves of past victories. Your current situation is not going to be solved in the future. It has already been solved in your past.

Armed only with his garment of praise and the sword of Goliath, David flees to the cave of Adullam. Starting over is never easy, but it is often of God. Covenant people go through many changes.

Word gets around that David has arrived in the cave, and people begin to gather themselves to him. David is wondering if his life is coming to an end, but covenant people cannot hide themselves and die. Their purpose is greater than death.

The last thing David thinks he needs at this point in his ministry is to be around all these new people. He misses Jonathan, his covenant brother. He is in constant danger because Saul wants to kill him. He has left everything and is in the process of starting over. He has no wealth, title, or position. He is depressed. But covenant is stronger than these kinds of circumstances.

David is not sure if he needs this flock that God has sent to walk with him. "And every one that was in distress, and every one that was in debt, and every one that was discontented, gathered themselves unto him; and he became a captain over them: and there were with him about four hundred men" (1 Sam. 22:2).

<hr />

David became the captain of about 400 misfits and *outcasts*. Yet, in his heart, he was still a shepherd. He was used to dealing with poor, helpless sheep. Indeed, being the sheep's helper had given him a reason to live in the past. This time would be no different. He was willing to *invest in these outcasts*. After all, what did he have to lose?

Distressed, in debt, and *discontented* were the words that described this new congregation, not to mention their pastor himself! These people were outcasts. David understood that *covenant people always invest in the outcast*. He had been an outcast before and had become one again.

Don't give up if you are a covenant man or woman. You may be in the starting-over phase of your life. Distressed, in debt, and discontented people may surround you, but you are still a giant-killer. You killed Goliath without a sword. You can certainly win this battle with Goliath's sword. The last time you faced an enemy larger than life, you had no sword. This time you are facing a more formidable foe—your own depression—and you have a giant sword. You are still a shepherd, and you are still a giant-killer.

As David pondered what to do with these outcasts, the prophet Gad came to his aid. In the times of your greatest distress, debt, and discontent, God will send a true prophetic word to you. This word will always tell you to move on and will encourage you to accomplish the impossible. A true word from God will always be greater than your current ability. If you have the ability to fulfill the word yourself, you will not need faith.

> *And the prophet Gad said unto David, Abide not in the hold; depart, and get thee into the land of Judah. Then David departed, and came into the forest of Hareth* (1 Samuel 22:5).

Gad's name meant "a great troop."[1] It was no accident that while David was surrounded by a group of *outcasts*, God sent a prophet with such a name. God caused David *to invest in the outcast* until they became a great troop. To do so, Gad said, "David, you cannot stay in the hold, but you must go to Judah." The hold is the place of "depression" and "despair." Judah is the place of "praise." To turn these *outcasts into a great troop*, he had to forget his circumstances and move to a place of praise!

If we stay in a holding position, looking at how distressed, in debt, and discontented we are—and the shape our flocks are in—we will never become a great troop. *Invest* some "Judah," some praise, *in the outcast* that God places in your life, and then watch the great transformation. Praise always produces greater results than worry.

David began *to invest in the outcast*. He took them to Judah as commanded. Meanwhile, Saul slew the entire priesthood in the house of Ahimelech because they had helped David. One of the sons of Ahimelech, named Abiathar, escaped and came to David in Judah (see 1 Sam. 22:18-23).

Abiathar by name means "abundance or father of plenty."[2] David had been faithful to stay in Judah and *invest in the outcasts* he had been given. Then God sent a man whose name meant abundance or father of plenty. If you can be faithful with the little that you have and stay in praise, God will send you abundance or plenty. These misfits were becoming a troop.

What a sad picture! Saul had killed the entire priesthood who stayed behind, and the only survivor fled and came to David in Judah. Ministry must move on or be killed by a religious order that rejects the changing of the day. This is no longer man's day. We are now in the Day of the Lord. We must go to our Beloved in a new place of praise. David was in Judah. Abiathar came with an ephod in his hand (see 1 Sam. 23:6). We must go to our Beloved with priestly ministry in our hands.

David's covenantal leadership transformed this outcast army into a great troop. They slew the Philistines in Keilah and saved the inhabitants thereof, returning from the battle with cattle and supplies. David had started over with a group of outcasts who had grown and prospered from 400 to 600 in a short time (see 1 Sam. 23:13). You can't stop the power of a covenant heart.

❋ ⟨⟨⟨⟩⟩⟩ ❋

Saul is hot on his trail, but David is hot after the purpose of God. The sweet psalmist continues to minister as a priest and a shepherd. He has *invested in the outcast,* and now God has rewarded him with a prosperous army. Be faithful to invest in the ones nobody wants, and God will be faithful to give you the ones everybody wants! But the ones everybody wishes they could have will be the same ones nobody wanted. They have been changed by the power of a covenant heart.

Endnotes

1. James Strong, *Strong's Exhaustive Concordance of the Bible* (Peabody, MA: Hendrickson Publishers, n.d.), **Gad**, H1408.

2. *Strong's*, **Ebyathar**, H54.

Old Testament Covenant Scriptures

Covenant Keeping May Mean Starting Over

David therefore departed thence, and escaped to the cave Adullam: and when his brethren and all his father's house heard it, they went down thither to him.

And every one that was in distress, and every one that was in debt, and every one that was discontented, gathered themselves unto him; and he became a captain over them: and there were with him about four hundred men (1 Samuel 22:1-2).

New Testament Applications

Jesus Invested in the Outcast

But when thou makest a feast, call the poor, the maimed, the lame, the blind (Luke 14:13).

Paul Invested in the Outcast

That I should be the minister of Jesus Christ to the Gentiles, ministering the gospel of God, that the offering up of the Gentiles might be acceptable, being sanctified by the Holy Ghost (Romans 15:16).

Chapter Nine

Covenant People Will Cover and Strengthen Each Other

David has started his ministry over again with nothing. His only parishioners are several hundred distressed, indebted, and discontented people. Saul has killed Ahimelech along with all the priests in his house who had served David communion bread and returned to him the sword of Goliath. But David the covenant man refuses to retaliate and fight Saul or defame him in any way.

Saul continues his search for David. God's chosen is hiding out with his new troop of former misfits in the wilderness and mountain strongholds of Ziph. Saul seeks him every day, but God will not allow Saul to find him (see 1 Sam. 23:14).

❦ ⌁⌁⌁ ❦

Ziph means "flowing,[1] or to soften[2] in the sun." When the enemies of your soul are out to kill you, God will prepare a table, a stronghold in the wilderness. There is a "Ziph" for each of us, a place where we soften in the presence of the Son and then are made ready to flow. There will be no flowing without a melting. The same fire that produces your flowing will first soften and melt you in order that He can mold you.

> *And the woman fled into the wilderness, where she hath a place prepared of God, that they should feed her there a thousand two hundred and threescore days* (Revelation 12:6).

> *And Jesus being full of the Holy Ghost returned from Jordan, and was led by the Spirit into the wilderness* (Luke 4:1).

The Pattern Son Himself had a wilderness experience. Jesus was in the wilderness for 40 days. The Old Testament church was in the wilderness for 40 years (see Acts 7:38). Which do you want? Every believer must have a wilderness experience, but that doesn't mean that you must have a wilderness wandering.

Covenant believers are no exception. The sun-clothed Woman, the Church who appears in Revelation 12:6, had a place prepared of God for her in the wilderness that she should be fed while the dragon sought to slay her. Jesus was led by the Spirit into the wilderness to be tempted of the devil. David had a prepared place in the wilderness of Ziph as Saul sought to tempt and slay him. That same kind of refuge is there for you and me.

David was weary from the battle at Keilah, not to mention Saul's dogged attempts to track him down and kill him. He was heartbroken that Saul's hatred of him had cost the priests of the Lord their lives. He felt alone, uncovered and weak, even among six hundred. David had submitted completely to Saul, and now his spiritual covering wanted him dead. He missed Jonathan, but how could Jonathan find him if Saul and all his army had not been able to find him? But the power of a covenant heart would prevail.

Saul and all his men could not search out David, though desperate to find and kill him. Yet, without effort, Jonathan went straight to David in the wilderness (see 1 Sam. 23:16). Covenant people know where their covenant partner can always be found.

You will not be able to hide from your covenant partner. They will know where you are and what you are feeling even when you think no one knows and no one cares. This is a heart connection. You are never without covering when you are in covenant.

Jonathan came to where David was and *covered and strengthened him*. David had been there for Jonathan when he needed him. Now Jonathan reciprocates the blessing. Covenant is not about who is over whom, or who submits to whom. Covenant is mutual respect, covering, and submission (see Eph. 5:21).

This covenant relationship between David and Jonathan was not between father and son. This kind of covenant was between womb brothers, companions in tribulation. It was at peer level, eyeball to eyeball. There is a great need for each of us to be covered from someone above us as a father or mentoring ministry. But just as vital is for each of us to have a peer-level covenantal companion for the purpose of *covering and strengthening each other*.

Jonathan found David when no one else could. He did not come to him as more than a friend, as a brother and companion. "And Jonathan Saul's son arose, and went to David into the wood, and strengthened his hand in God" (1 Sam. 23:16).

When no one else knows where we are and what we are feeling, our covenant partners will be able to find us and discern our feelings. However, we should also learn to swallow our pride and make our feelings and needs known. We often wait on someone to discern our places of hiding when God is melting our pride and softening us to cause us to admit we need each other. Covenant people *cover and strengthen each other*.

Jonathan promised that Saul would not find David, and committed to David that Jesse's shepherd-son would be the next king over Israel (see 1 Sam. 23:17). What covenant! The son of Saul was devoted to someone else being king instead of himself. He further stated that he would be next to David when he reigned. That is what tormented Saul, that covenant was thicker than natural blood.

David had been weakened from constant battle, but just a few private moments with his covenant brother and companion had *strengthened him*. He no longer felt naked and ashamed. Jonathan had *covered and strengthened him* in his moment of weakness.

If you are tired and weary from the battle of religious politics and from the carnal warfare of flesh, make some time for those you have covenant with. You will not only be refreshed, you will be *covered and strengthened* for the next battle you face.

❀ ⌐⟶ ❀

The two covenant partners make a fresh covenant before the Lord. David stays in the wilderness, and Jonathan returns to his house. The power of a covenant heart not only will find your companion in their wilderness, but it will not leave them in the same condition as you found them. David is left *covered and strengthened*.

Rest assured that every covenant person eventually finds himself or herself in a wilderness called Ziph. You may think that God has brought you there to kill you. Well, He has! He has brought you there to kill your pride, your limited wisdom and strength, that He might live through you. This is not your ending. It is just your softening so that there can be His flowing out of you. You will not be delivered into the hand of Saul. You will leave this wilderness stronghold *covered and strengthened*!

Endnotes

1. James Strong, *Strong's Exhaustive Concordance of the Bible* (Peabody, MA: Hendrickson Publishers, n.d.), **Ziypt**, H2128.

2. *Strong's*, **Zepheth**, H2203.

Old Testament Covenant Scriptures

Covenant Keeping Involves a Wilderness Experience

And David abode in the wilderness in strong holds, and remained in a mountain in the wilderness of Ziph. And Saul sought him every day, but God delivered him not into his hand.

And David saw that Saul was come out to seek his life: and David was in the wilderness of Ziph in a wood (1 Samuel 23:14-15).

Covenant People Receive Strength in the Wilderness

And Jonathan Saul's son arose, and went to David into the wood, and strengthened his hand in God.

And he said unto him, Fear not: for the hand of Saul my father shall not find thee; and thou shalt be king over Israel, and I shall be next unto thee; and that also Saul my father knoweth.

And they two made a covenant before the Lord: and David abode in the wood, and Jonathan went to his house (1 Samuel 23:16-18).

New Testament Applications

Jesus Strengthened Peter and Commanded Him to Strengthen Others

And the Lord said, Simon, Simon, behold, satan hath desired to have you, that he may sift you as wheat: but I have prayed for thee, that thy faith fail not: and when thou art converted, strengthen thy brethren (Luke 22:31-32).

Paul Taught That We Are to Strengthen One Another

Brethren, if a man be overtaken in a fault, ye which are spiritual, restore such an one in the spirit of meekness; considering thyself, lest thou also be tempted. Bear ye one another's burdens, and so fulfil the law of Christ (Galatians 6:1).

Chapter Ten

Covenant People Will Never Betray Those Over Them in the Lord

The battle rages on in the heart of Saul. He wants his young rival dead, pursuing after David wherever he goes. Every move David and his rag-tag army make, he can be assured that Saul is lurking near to seek his life.

Saul has now gathered three thousand men to assist him in tracking down David. By now David is dwelling in the strongholds of the wilderness of Engedi, so Saul follows him there.

David and his men are in a large cave in Engedi. The sovereign God has such a sense of humor. As Saul passes by, he has to use the bathroom, and chooses David's hideout as the place to relieve himself (see 1 Sam. 24:3). As Saul is disrobed to do his business, David's men encourage him to kill Saul while he is in such a vulnerable position.

David has never considered harming Saul. In fact, David has never thought of saying an evil word against his adversary. David is a covenant man. *Covenant people never betray those over them in the Lord.*

❊ ⌐▀▄▀▄⌐ ❊

Saul had lied to David over and over again. He had thrown the javelin at him more than one time. He had ruined his name and reputation. He had poisoned his wife against him, and then he had mobilized an army to track him down like a wild animal that needed to be killed. Yet, David *could not betray the one over him in the Lord.*

How could David still regard this man as the Lord's anointed after all this? The power of a covenant heart is not only forgiving; it is also wise. If it had not been for Saul, David would probably have been a Saul himself. The "Saul" inside of David had to die as well. They didn't need another madman on the throne. Saul's abuse and betrayal had made David covenantal.

In a moment of weakness and at the encouragement of his own men, David slipped up behind Saul and quietly cut off the skirt of his robe (see 1 Sam. 24:4). As David's men prepared to slay Saul, the covenant heart in David convicted him of his actions. David then repented of his thoughts to harm the king (see 1 Sam. 24:5).

> *And he said unto his men, The Lord forbid that I should do this thing unto my master, the Lord's anointed, to stretch forth mine hand against him, seeing he is the anointed of the Lord* (1 Samuel 24:6).

Amazingly, David still regarded Saul as his master and the anointed of the Lord. Many people will never understand the power of a covenant heart until they understand how much God honors authority. *Covenant will never allow you to betray those that are in authority.*

74

> *Everyone must submit himself to the governing authorities, for there is no authority except that which God has established. The authorities that exist have been established by God* (Romans 13:1 NIV).

Even the rulers of the natural realm are ministers of God ordained for our good. If we resist them, we resist the ordinances of God. In Romans 9:16-18, Paul declared that God raised up Pharaoh for His own purposes that He might show His power in him, that the name of the Lord might be declared in all the earth. If God respects the authority of natural leaders, even corrupt men like Pharaoh and Saul, we should have no problem submitting to and honoring godly leaders (see Heb. 13:7,17).

David never sought to justify wrong behavior because of the evil actions of Saul. Covenant does not fight fire with fire. If God placed you with or under a person who is not your ideal of a perfect leader, know that God is using him or her to work something into you and out of you. The question is, "Did God put you with this leader?" What God "hath joined together, let not man put asunder" (Mt. 19:6b). The New American Standard Version says, "Let no man separate."

God not only honors authority, He honors those who honor authority. Covenant people do not discredit those who are in authority, even those in natural places of authority. You can disagree and address issues without slandering the authority. The position should be respected even if the person holding the position has lost respectability. *Covenant people never disrespect authority.*

To show the full extent of God's respect for authority, pay attention to Jude 9.

> *Yet Michael the archangel, when contending with the devil he disputed about the body of Moses, durst not bring against him a railing accusation, but said, The Lord rebuke thee* (Jude 1:9).

If God did not allow Michael to bring a railing accusation against the devil, He certainly will not allow such finger-pointing against your set, chosen, and appointed leader.

Some may read these words and think that I am encouraging abuse. But you did not pick your leader. God gave them to you. I do not believe we have the right to choose churches and pastors—God appoints them (Ps. 68:6; 1 Cor. 12:18,28). Most abuse comes from being in the wrong place under the wrong leadership. If you are where God placed you and under the one God placed over you, then God will use the good, the bad, and the ugly to make a David out of you instead of a Saul. Remember that God used Saul to help mold David's covenant heart.

As Saul pulled up his skirt and prepared to leave the cave, he had no idea that his backside was showing. Every leader has a backside, and if you stay around long enough, you will surely see it. This was not the first time David had seen the worst of Saul, but the covenant heart in David would not allow anyone else to see Saul uncovered for what he really was.

> And David said to Saul, Wherefore hearest thou men's words, saying, Behold, David seeketh thy hurt? Behold, this day thine eyes have seen how that the Lord had delivered thee today into mine hand in the cave: and some bade me kill thee: but mine eye spared thee; and I said, I will not put forth mine hand against my lord; for he is the Lord's anointed (1 Samuel 24:9-10).

David assured Saul that he had not sinned against him, nor would he sin against him. Saul wept when David called him his father. Fathers do not always behave like fathers. God does not always give us what we want but rather what we need. It was not Moses who was responsible for Israel crossing the Red Sea, but Pharaoh. It was not Jesse who was responsible for David. It was Saul who really made David great.

And he said to David, Thou art more righteous than I: for thou hast rewarded me good, whereas I have rewarded thee evil (1 Samuel 24:17).

The power of a covenant heart can melt the heart of a jealous king. Saul admitted that God had given David the throne, but made David swear that he would not cut off his seed or his name out of Israel. David was a covenant man. He *would never betray Saul or his seed after him.* David held no malice in his heart against Saul. David honored authority.

There is no justification for abusive leadership; likewise, there is no justification for rebellion against authority. "Rebellion is as the sin of witchcraft" (1 Sam. 15:23a). *Covenant people never betray those over them in the Lord.*

But Saul's anger and rage soon returned, and once again he sought for David's life. The religious system can only stay sincere as long as their life depends on it. When death is no longer a threat, they return to their old habits and traditions and methods. They are addicted to hard, sin-conscious preaching. Covenant theology full of grace and truth makes no sense to them.

God tested His man again. A second time David was given opportunity to kill Saul. A deep sleep fell upon Saul and his men. David took the sword of Saul while Saul slept and then awakened the evil king to show him that again he had refused *to betray the one over him in the Lord* (see 1 Sam. 26:7-25).

Learn David's covenantal secret. His greatness was determined by his attitude toward his enemies! In his own words of testimony, he declared, "Thou hast also given me the shield of Thy salvation: and Thy right hand hath holden me up, and Thy gentleness hath made me great" (Ps. 18:35).

Saul has become so distraught at this point that he seeks the aid of a witch at Endor to call up the spirit of Samuel (see 1 Sam. 28:5-25). The old order that has rejected the ministry of the Holy Spirit has a date with a witch! Fleshly, religious systems, desperate for what covenant people have, are seeking out false prophets, fortune-tellers, and scam artists to keep them alive. But there are no answers from the dead. Even the familiar spirit tells Saul that God has chosen David!

Through every circumstance, David *never betrays Saul. David always regards Saul as the anointed of the Lord.* David knows that the Lord will deal with Saul in His own time and in His own way (see 1 Sam. 26:10). It is not our responsibility to correct those over us in the Lord. It is only our responsibility to correct our attitudes toward them.

Old Testament Covenant Scriptures

Covenant People Honor Authority

And he said unto his men, The Lord forbid that I should do this thing unto my master, the Lord's anointed, to stretch forth mine hand against him, seeing he is the anointed of the Lord.

And David said to Saul, Wherefore hearest thou men's words, saying, Behold, David seeketh thy hurt?

Behold, this day thine eyes have seen how that the Lord had delivered thee today into mine hand in the cave: and some bade me kill thee: but mine eye spared thee; and I said, I will not put forth mine hand against my lord; for he is the Lord's anointed (1 Samuel 24:6,9-10).

Covenant People Return Good for Evil

And he said to David, Thou art more righteous than I: for thou hast rewarded me good, whereas I have rewarded thee evil.

And thou hast showed this day how that thou hast dealt well with me: forasmuch as when the Lord had delivered me into thine hand, thou killedst me not (1 Samuel 24:17-18).

New Testament Applications

Jesus Never Betrayed His Father

Then said Jesus unto them, When ye have lifted up the Son of man, then shall ye know that I am He, and that I do nothing of Myself; but as My Father hath taught Me, I speak these things (John 8:28).

Paul Taught That We Are to Obey Those Over Us in the Lord

Obey them that have the rule over you, and submit yourselves: for they watch for your souls, as they that must give account, that they may do it with joy, and not with grief: for that is unprofitable for you (Hebrews 13:17).

Chapter Eleven

Covenant People Will Encourage Themselves in the Lord

Victories are being won at every turn in the life of the shepherd-king. Finally, things seem to be "looking up" for David. His army of former outcasts has proven to be quite a force to be reckoned with. God has delivered Saul into his hand twice, and given him the grace to spare his enemy.

But as David's band heads for the comfort zone of home base in Ziklag, they see and smell smoke. Fear grips their hearts as they discover what could only be described as a nightmare. In their absence, the Amalekites have invaded their city, burned it with fire, and taken their wives and children captive. The first question in their minds is, "How can this be?"

Covenant people face similar challenges. While doing the work they are called and chosen for, their enemies sometimes invade their homes, businesses, churches, or communities to seek and put their loved ones in bondage. Discouragement is a strong demonic device.

Then David and the people that were with him lifted up their voice and wept, until they had no more power to weep (1 Samuel 30:4).

Even covenant people will have seasons of weeping. You may see every prayer you pray for someone else's family answered while your own family seemingly grows worse. You may speak a word into a congregation that brings instant change and renewal while your own local congregation seems to dwindle. You may watch every business in town prosper as your own is faced with debt. Just when David thinks it can not get any worse, it does.

And David was greatly distressed; for the people spake of stoning him, because the soul of all the people was grieved, every man for his sons and for his daughters: but David encouraged himself in the Lord his God (1 Samuel 30:6).

In his moment of distress, David makes a decision not to be discouraged but rather *to encourage himself in the Lord.*

❉ ⟲⟳ ❉

The man or woman of covenant understands that anything that has the power to shake his or her confidence is not of God. David knew from past hurts and battles that tough times would not last forever, but tough people could and would survive the strongest test. Sitting on a pile of ashes and burnt stones, David realized that discouragement was a taller giant than Goliath. Yet, he knew for a fact that giants do die. From that same pile of ashes, *David encouraged himself in the Lord.*

David called for Abiathar the priest, Ahimelech's son, to bring him the linen ephod. It was Abiathar who had run into the camp when David was distressed and surrounded by hurting people after Saul decreed to have him killed. David learned then that the power of praise would turn his captivity. He again put on the linen ephod, the garment of praise for his spirit of heaviness (see Is. 61:3). He *was encouraging himself in the Lord.*

David's family had been taken captive, his adopted home had been burned with fire, and now his own men were thinking of stoning him. David called for Abiathar and the garment of praise (see 1 Sam. 30:7). He was about to praise his way out of discouragement. There are times when no one will encourage you, so you must learn *to encourage yourself in the Lord.*

To be faced with as many disappointments as David faced would cause some to give up in despair or become addicted to their trials. Without a covenant heart, people stop pressing. They soon begin to pity themselves and start creating their own problems. Without a covenant heart, people worship their fiery trials. Don't waste your sorrows on unnecessary things. *Encourage yourself in the Lord.*

When David was running from Saul without food or a weapon, he ran to the house of the priest and was given the linen ephod of priestly ministry, communion bread, and the sword of Goliath. Once again, he is running, but this time it is from his own discouragement, and the priest again brings him the linen ephod. We must learn to praise God, not because we feel like it, but because He is God. Then we will conquer every foe that rises against us from within or without. We must learn *to encourage ourselves in the Lord.*

David worshiped and praised his way out of despair. His men were no help, held fast in the clutches of helpless depression. Nothing in the natural had changed, but something inside David had changed. He was a covenant man, and he knew that the things that are seen are temporal, but the things that are not seen are eternal (see 2 Cor. 4:18). David was encouraged by the power of praise.

> *And David inquired at the Lord, saying, Shall I pursue after this troop? shall I overtake them? And He answered him, Pursue: for thou shalt surely overtake them, and without fail recover all* (1 Samuel 30:8).

You cannot recover if you remain in discouragement. *Recover* is an interesting word. It implies taking back into possession what is lost, but also suggests covering again. To be *re*-covered is to be brought back under covering again. This is a day to take back into your possession everything that has been burned, destroyed, or taken by your enemies. One vital key is to come back under the covering that God has placed over you.

David may have been sitting on a pile of ashes in Ziklag, but he had Zion beating in his covenant heart. He was ready to rescue his family and restore his city. Are you ready to pursue, overtake, and without fail recover it all? Then start right now by *encouraging yourself in the Lord.*

When two hundred of the six hundred men with David became too faint to go up against the Amalekites, David continued to *encourage himself in the Lord*. He found a young Egyptian servant of the Amalekites who led him into the enemy's camp (see 1 Sam. 30:13-17). David and his four hundred men smote the enemy from the morning to the evening. David rescued his family and brought revenge on the Amalekites.

> *And there was nothing lacking to them, neither small nor great, neither sons nor daughters, neither spoil, nor any thing that they had taken to them: David recovered all* (1 Samuel 30:19).

If you find yourself sitting on a pile of ashes, and your family is in captivity, and the men that you thought were with you are thinking to stone you to death, don't just sit there singing the blues. Jesus in you is alive and well. Put on your garment of praise. You are about to pursue, overtake, and without fail recover all. The power of a covenant heart will lift you from tragedy to triumph.

David recovered all. What a powerful statement! If it happened for David, it can happen for you. God is no respecter of persons (see Acts 10:34). *Encourage yourself in the Lord.*

❦ ⟶ ❦

David returns from Ziklag with far more than he lost. He returns with what was taken but also with the spoils of the Amalekites. He has pursued, overtaken, and recovered all. The secret of his success is not his ability to fight. When total loss and destruction are all that he can see, his secret is to lift his eyes higher into the heavens and focus on Zion. *He encourages himself in the Lord.*

Old Testament Covenant Scriptures

Covenant People Will Experience Tribulation

So David and his men came to the city, and, behold, it was burned with fire; and their wives, and their sons, and their daughters, were taken captives.

Then David and the people that were with him lifted up their voice and wept, until they had no more power to weep.

And David's two wives were taken captives, Ahinoam the Jezreelitess, and Abigail the wife of Nabal the Carmelite (1 Samuel 30:3-5).

Covenant People Turn to God Even in the Midst of Tribulation

And David was greatly distressed; for the people spake of stoning him, because the soul of all the people was grieved, every man for his sons and for his daughters: but David encouraged himself in the Lord his God.

And David inquired at the Lord, saying, Shall I pursue after this troop? shall I overtake them? And He answered him, Pursue: for thou shalt surely overtake them, and without fail recover all (1 Samuel 30:6,8).

New Testament Applications

Jesus Encouraged Himself and Others

These things have I spoken unto you, that My joy might remain in you, and that your joy might be full (John 15:11).

Paul Encouraged Himself and Others

Rejoice in the Lord alway: and again I say, Rejoice (Philippians 4:4).

Chapter Twelve

Covenant People Value Relationships More Than Everything

Nothing means more to a man or woman of covenant than the relationships God has ordained for their lives. David is no exception. Even his fondness for Saul remains intact. The love David has for Jonathan has been evident since the day they entered into covenant. His fondness and love are never more evident than on the day he receives word of Saul and Jonathan's death.

David has just returned from the victory over the Amalekites with two days at home in Ziklag to rest and rejoice in the victory. On the morning of the third day, a young Amalekite runs into the camp with the crown and bracelet of Saul to give as a gift to David. David says, "Tell me, how went the matter?"

The young man replies, "The people are fled and many are dead including Saul and his son Jonathan" (see 2 Sam. 1:3-4). The young man falsely explains that he had come upon Saul, who had already been wounded in the battle, and that Saul had asked him to kill him to put him out of his misery. The young man, using Saul's own sword, had killed the jealous king. Now this Amalekite is bringing Saul's crown and bracelet to David with great pride and arrogance.

David is unimpressed. Rather than rejoice over the end of his tribulations, he rends his clothes and mourns, weeps, and fasts until evening (see 2 Sam. 1:11-12). The young man is confused; he thought David would be happy that his enemy was dead. But David's covenant heart knows Saul was not his enemy—he had been his mentor. Saul viewed David as an enemy, but David saw Saul as a father. Jonathan was his womb brother and companion in tribulation, and now he is dead. David weeps and mourns and cannot eat because *he values relationships more than everything*. Now, two of his most important relationships are dead.

Covenant people never rejoice over the death or struggles of another believer, even if that believer has persecuted them or sought to destroy them. Covenant people understand that there is a blessing for those who are persecuted by others who are used by God to test them. If it were not for Saul, David would have not met Jonathan. If it were not for Saul, David could have turned out exactly like his tormentor. David sent for the young Amalekite.

> *And David said unto him, How wast thou not afraid to stretch forth thine hand to destroy the Lord's anointed?* (2 Samuel 1:14)

After all that Saul had done to destroy David, David still regarded him as the Lord's anointed. David called for one of his men to kill the Amalekite for having killed Saul. David told the young man, "Your blood be upon you, because your mouth has testified against you saying that you have slain the Lord's anointed" (see 2 Sam. 1:16). After all this suffering, David still *valued relationships more than everything*.

> *And David lamented with this lamentation over Saul and over Jonathan his son* (2 Samuel 1:17).

David cried out for Judah to teach the children the use of the "bow" (the title of his dirge) and not allow the memory of these two great men to be forgotten. He lamented, "How are the mighty fallen?" He instructed that it not be told in Gath or published in their streets lest the Philistines rejoice. He cursed the mountains of Gilboa, the place of their death. He proclaimed that there would not be rain or dew upon them. David declared Saul and Jonathan lovely and pleasant in life and undivided in death, and announced that they were swifter than eagles and stronger than lions. Finally, he told the daughters of Israel to weep and honor Saul for his previous kindness upon them (see 2 Sam. 1:18-24). Afterwards, in great contriteness of spirit, he began to weep for himself.

> *How are the mighty fallen in the midst of the battle! O Jonathan, thou wast slain in thine high places. I am distressed for thee, my brother Jonathan: very pleasant hast thou been unto me: thy love to me was wonderful, passing the love of women. How are the mighty fallen, and the weapons of war perished!* (2 Samuel 1:25-27)

※ ～～～ ※

David has been on a constant, emotional roller coaster since we first met him as a young shepherd boy. He was the leader of Saul's army and then found himself running from that army in fear of his life. He started over in the cave with a group of misfits and outcasts. This group became great and then discovered everything they owned had been stolen or burned. They recovered all and thought things were going their way. Now, death has come to his mentor and covenant brother. No battle yet has been so tough

91

as the battle he faces in his own emotions. He *values these relation-ships more than everything.*

He *values these relationships* so much that he has the young man put to death who claimed to have killed Saul. We must slay everything in us which is not covenantal. We must eliminate every-thing that hinders us from walking in covenant with each other. Any enemy of covenant that we let live today will betray us tomor-row. Nothing is more important than our covenant relationships.

Our greatest challenge is to so *value covenant relationships* that we can still regard as the anointed of the Lord those that use and abuse us. God honors relationships, and it is time that we honored them as well.

Old Testament Covenant Scriptures

Covenant People Honor Departed Leaders

And David said unto him, How wast thou not afraid to stretch forth thine hand to destroy the Lord's anointed?

And David called one of the young men, and said, Go near, and fall upon him. And he smote him that he died.

And David said unto him, Thy blood be upon thy head; for thy mouth hath testified against thee, saying, I have slain the Lord's anointed.

And David lamented with this lamentation over Saul and over Jonathan his son (2 Samuel 1:14-17).

Covenant Love Transcends Death

Saul and Jonathan were lovely and pleasant in their lives, and in their death they were not divided: they were swifter than eagles, they were stronger than lions.

How are the mighty fallen in the midst of the battle! O Jonathan, thou wast slain in thine high places.

I am distressed for thee, my brother Jonathan: very pleasant hast thou been unto me: thy love to me was wonderful, passing the love of women.

How are the mighty fallen, and the weapons of war perished! (2 Samuel 1:23, 25-27)

New Testament Applications

Jesus Valued Relationships

This is My commandment, That ye love one another, as I have loved you.

Greater love hath no man than this, that a man lay down his life for his friends.

Ye are My friends, if ye do whatsoever I command you (John 15:12-14).

Paul Valued Relationships

Submitting yourselves one to another in the fear of God (Ephesians 5:21).

Chapter Thirteen

Covenant People Desire to Bless Their Own Household

There is something about death that makes a person question and prioritize everything. David continues to mourn his loss and to plan for his future. While David prays through his pain, the Lord speaks to him to take his family and go up to Hebron. While there, the men of the tribe of Judah come and anoint him king over the house of Judah. Even in the midst of death, God is prospering the destiny He has placed on David.

It is told to David that the men of Jabesh-gilead have buried Saul. David, still desiring to honor Saul, enters into covenant with these men to show kindness to them for what they have done for Saul. One of Saul's sons, Ishbosheth, refuses to acknowledge David as king and assumes the kingship over Israel.

The name *Ishbosheth* comes from two Hebrew words, the first meaning "man,"[1] and the second meaning "shame and confusion."[2] This son of Saul is a man of shame and confusion. The only thing religion can produce is shame and confusion. David is the opposite. He is a man of covenant, producing confidence and understanding. It is also interesting that Ishbosheth's name is akin to the meaning of the name for Goliath that we dealt with in a previous chapter.

Now there was long war between the house of Saul and the house of David: but David waxed stronger and stronger, and the house of Saul waxed weaker and weaker (2 Samuel 3:1).

David has just turned 30 years old, yet has already lived a lifetime of experiences that most men double his age will never know. He has demonstrated remarkable maturity beyond his years, a prototype of a genuine covenant man. King David will reign seven years and six months over Judah and thirty-three years over all of Israel and Judah. His top priority now is to be faithful to the legacy of Saul and *to bless his own household*. He has not seen Michal since the night he was forced to flee the wrath of Saul. He is ready to reunite his family. David has Michal returned to him while in Hebron.

Ishbosheth continued to fight against David until he was killed as he slept upon his bed (see 2 Sam. 4:7). The men who killed Ishbosheth brought his head to David, hoping that he would be proud of them. But David did to them as he had done to the Amalekite who had killed Saul. They were killed for slaying the anointed of the Lord. David never ceased to operate in covenant, even after the death of Saul. He continued to honor Saul and the seed of Saul after him.

It was David's desire to fetch the Ark of the Covenant back to Jerusalem and to allow the glory of God to return to his city. He gathered thirty thousand chosen men and went to recapture the presence of God. He placed the Ark on the back of a new cart pulled by oxen. All went well until they reached the threshing floor, and the oxen began to stumble and to shake the Ark. Uzzah put forth his hand to steady the Ark, and God smote him. Uzzah died there on the threshing floor. David was afraid to move the Ark, so he parked it in the house of Obededom the Gittite for three months.

> *And it was told king David, saying, The Lord hath blessed the house of Obededom, and all that pertaineth unto him, because of the ark of God. So David went and brought up the ark of God from the house of Obededom into the city of David with gladness* (2 Samuel 6:12).

David had mistakenly thought that the reason Uzzah had been killed was because the Ark was cursed. But the real reason was the method they were using to transport it. They were carrying the Ark on a new cart. The new cart was made up of wood boards and two big wheels pulled by oxen. The Ark of God had always been destined to be shouldered on the back of a priesthood that is committed and under command—a priesthood sanctified by blood and oil (see Ex. 28).

Modern Christendom makes the same mistakes. Men come up with new programs to bring in the presence of God, and we appoint boards made up of mostly big wheels to determine the will of God. All these concepts are pulled by the beastly mind-sets of carnal logic, a carbon copy of Philistine methodology (see 1 Sam. 6). David finally figured out that the priests must bear on their shoulders the glory of God as they began anew to return the Ark into the city of David. There was great rejoicing. David took off his dignified robe and danced with all his might in the Holy Ghost. He was restoring the power of God's presence and the glory of God to his city, and it was in his heart *to bless his household.*

> *And as the ark of the Lord came into the city of David, Michal Saul's daughter looked through a window, and saw king David leaping and dancing before the Lord; and she despised him in her heart* (2 Samuel 6:16).

The whole city rejoiced with David, celebrating the return of God's presence to Jerusalem. Second Samuel 6:20 shows that after the entire fanfare was over, David departed from the crowd to his own abode with the *desire to bless his own household*. But Michal met him with criticism and mockery. She sounded a lot like her father, more interested in public appearances than true worship.

David told her he had come home *to bless her*, but her attitude toward fresh praise and worship hindered her ability to receive. He also made it clear that he was not going to apologize for his freedom in worship, because it was before and unto the Lord that he danced, and he would become even more "vile than thus" (see 2 Sam. 6:20-21). The next verse is a sad statement about those who refuse to embrace the fresh move of God.

> *Therefore Michal the daughter of Saul had no child unto the day of her death* (2 Samuel 6:23).

Covenant people *desire to bless their own household* but cannot be responsible for the refusal of their own to accept the blessing. There are times that the whole city may rejoice with you, and your own household scorn what God is doing in you and through you. Don't stop dancing before the Lord. Even if your own family does not understand, keep *desiring to bless them*. If they do not embrace the move of God, they will be barren and never produce the presence of God.

David loves Michal and wants *to bless her*, but she has too much of her father and the old order left in her. What people think is still important to the house and lineage of Saul. Michal is worried about public approval of the king's actions instead of the approval of God. Her unwillingness to change and submit causes her permanent barrenness. Always be willing *to bless your own household*, but remember they will never produce unless they change and submit to the Lord. Keep dancing. Don't allow the unfruitful to steal your joy and fruit. *David returned to bless his own household*. He left the results in the hands of God.

You cannot be responsible for your own household's attitude toward you, but you can and must be responsible for your attitude toward your household. Never let their negativity change your *desire to bless them.*

Endnotes

1. James Strong, *Strong's Exhaustive Concordance of the Bible* (Peabody, MA: Hendrickson Publishers, n.d.), **eesh**, #376.

2. *Strong's*, **eesh Bosheth**, #378.

Old Testament Covenant Scriptures

David Desired to Bless His Household

And as the ark of the Lord came into the city of David, Michal Saul's daughter looked through a window, and saw king David leaping and dancing before the Lord; and she despised him in her heart.

Then David returned to bless his household. And Michal the daughter of Saul came out to meet David, and said, How glorious was the king of Israel today, who uncovered himself today in the eyes of the handmaids of his servants, as one of the vain fellows shamelessly uncovereth himself! (2 Samuel 6:16,20)

Covenant People Desire to Please God Rather Than Man

And David said unto Michal, It was before the Lord, which chose me before thy father, and before all his house, to appoint me ruler over the people of the Lord, over Israel: therefore will I play before the Lord.

And I will yet be more vile than thus, and will be base in mine own sight: and of the maidservants which thou hast spoken of, of them shall I be had in honour.

Therefore Michal the daughter of Saul had no child unto the day of her death (2 Samuel 6:21-23).

New Testament Applications

Jesus Desired to Bless His Mother

Then saith He to the disciple, Behold thy mother! And from that hour that disciple took her unto his own home (John 19:27).

Paul Taught That We Are to Bless Our Household

But if any provide not for his own, and specially for those of his own house, he hath denied the faith, and is worse than an infidel (1 Timothy 5:8).

For the unbelieving husband is sanctified by the wife, and the unbelieving wife is sanctified by the husband: else were your children unclean; but now are they holy (1 Corinthians 7:14).

Chapter Fourteen

Covenant People Will Commit to Each Other's Seed

Finally, a season of peace comes to David's life. While resting from war with his enemies, he has more time to meditate and think. He really misses Jonathan, his covenant brother. He had promised Saul that he would always honor his seed. He has been faithful to do that even when the seed of Saul has not honored him. David is lonely. Michal has not shared his purpose. She is more like her father. If only Jonathan was still alive.

At this same time, a young cripple is hiding away in a place called Lodebar. He is the son of Jonathan and the grandson of Saul. This young man is even lonelier than David is. He is afraid of David. Because he is a descendant of Saul, he is convinced that David will have him killed.

Often the things or people we are afraid of are the very things or ones who bring fulfillment into our lives. David needs this young crippled man, and this young crippled man needs David.

While David rests, God sends Nathan the prophet to him with a message. God says, "If you will build Me a house, then I will build you a house." God further promises to establish the throne of David with his seed after him (see 2 Sam. 7:11-13). The words of Nathan remind David of his covenant with Jonathan. *David is committed to Jonathan's seed.* Now, the new king is dedicated to building God a house.

❀ ⌘ ❀

Once again there was warfare (see 2 Sam. 8:1-18). (Every time you commit to build the house of God or to fulfill His plan, there will be warfare. Don't stop building.) After the battle was won, the first phrase out of the mouth of David was concerning his covenant with Jonathan.

> *And David said, Is there yet any that is left of the house of Saul, that I may show him kindness for Jonathan's sake?* (2 Samuel 9:1)

Ziba, a servant of Saul, told David about Mephibosheth, the crippled son of Jonathan. The young lad was terrified of the thought of David, not knowing of the covenant between his father and David. Mephibosheth had been crippled since the day Jonathan and Saul were killed in battle. Upon discovery of their deaths, Mephibosheth's nurse ran with the five-year-old child in her arms. As she stumbled, the little boy fell from her arms and broke both his ankles (see 2 Sam. 4:4).

Until the day David sent for him, Mephibosheth was left at a place called Lodebar. *Lodebar* by definition means "the place of no pasture, no word or communication."[1] From the day he was left fatherless, Mephibosheth had been in a place of no communication.

How many people today have been dropped, crippled in their walk with God because no one has communicated to them that they have a covenant with the King? Mephibosheth was as lame from his lack of knowledge as he was from his infirmity (see Hos. 4:6). No one had told him that broken bones could heal.

When sent for, Mephibosheth entered the house of the king with great insecurity, fearing for his very life. The lame grandson of Saul had no idea of the covenant that he had with David. He did not know that he had been blessed with a covenant that had been established before he had been born!

And he bowed himself, and said, What is thy servant, that thou shouldest look upon such a dead dog as I am? (2 Samuel 9:8)

So many saints today are isolated, left alone in their fear because no one has communicated to them the good news. A covenant with the King was established long before they were born. They will remain in these out-of-the-way places of their own depression, simply existing below their predestined privileges. They will remain crippled in their walk until they leave Lodebar and join themselves to the house of the King. Once safely there, they will sit as a King's son at His table for the rest of their days. The linen cloth that drapes His table will forever cover their crippled condition (see Rev. 19:8)!

David and Jonathan cut a covenant that extended beyond themselves. *They committed to each other's seed.* Their covenant agreement was, "The Lord be between me and thee, and between my seed and thy seed for ever" (1 Sam. 20:42). For years after the death of Jonathan, David was still holding true to his covenant with the seed of Jonathan.

...As for Mephibosheth, said the king, he shall eat at my table, as one of the king's sons (2 Samuel 9:11).

True covenant men and women are committed *to each other's seed.* If the enemy cannot get the covenant parents to feud with each other, he will try to bring division through their children. As adults, we are in covenant with one another. That covenant extends to our children. Do not allow your sons and daughters to fuss and feud with each other, because our covenant is also with *each other's seed.*

David kept his covenant with Jonathan by showing favor to Mephibosheth. He also kept his word to Saul by showing favor to Ziba, the servant of Saul. The power of a covenant heart will not allow you to dishonor your word or break covenant. The power of a covenant heart will cause us to *commit to each other's seed.*

This is not the end of the commitment to the seed of Jonathan. Later in Second Samuel 21, to break the force of famine that was caused by Saul's breaking covenant with the Gibeonites, seven of the descendants of Saul were required to be killed on a tree. David took the two sons of Rizpah and the five grandsons that Michal had raised and offered them on the tree. But he spared Mephibosheth the son of Jonathan because of the covenant he had with Jonathan (see 2 Sam. 21:7). *Covenant people are committed to each other's seed.*

It had not rained for three years because of broken covenant between Saul and the Gibeonites. When we break covenant, we will go through a famine. The only thing that could break the famine was the death of *seven* of Saul's descendants on a tree. Our famine was ended when He who was *seven* died on the tree forever reversing the broken covenant of Adam—His crucifixion was the *perfect* hanging, once and for all! *Seven* is the number of completion and perfection.

❧ ⌁ ❧

Rizpah, the concubine of Saul, spreads sackcloth on the rock in front of where her sons are killed, refusing to sleep or eat as she fights the birds and beasts off her dead children's bodies (see 2 Sam. 21:10). They have been put to death at the beginning of barley harvest. Similarly, our harvest began with a death on a tree. Rizpah stays on the rock until the rain comes. May we abide on the Rock until the rain comes!

When it begins to rain, King David is told what Rizpah has done. Her actions move the heart of the King to give her children a proper burial. Moreover, he takes back the bones of Saul and Jonathan from the Philistines and gives them a proper burial as well (see 2 Sam. 21:13-14). *Covenant people are committed to each other's seed.*

What we need today are those like Rizpah, covenant people who will stay on the Rock and fight off the birds and the beasts from their seed until the rain comes down from Heaven. We need covenant people who will stay on the Rock until the heart of the King is moved. We need covenant people who will stay on the Rock until an old dead order that does not practice and understand covenant is buried forever. Stay on the Rock!

Endnote

1. James Strong, *Strong's Exhaustive Concordance of the Bible* (Peabody, MA: Hendrickson Publishers, n.d.), **Lo' Debav**, H3810.

Old Testament Covenant Scriptures

Covenant People Honor Commitments

And Jonathan, Saul's son, had a son that was lame of his feet. He was five years old when the tidings came of Saul and Jonathan out of Jezreel, and his nurse took him up, and fled: and it came to pass, as she made haste to flee, that he fell, and became lame. And his name was Mephibosheth (2 Samuel 4:4).

And David said, Is there yet any that is left of the house of Saul, that I may show him kindness for Jonathan's sake?

And the king said, Is there not yet any of the house of Saul, that I may show the kindness of God unto him? And Ziba said unto the king, Jonathan hath yet a son, which is lame on his feet.

And the king said unto him, Where is he? And Ziba said unto the king, Behold, he is in the house of Machir, the son of Ammiel, in Lodebar.

Then king David sent, and fetched him out of the house of Machir, the son of Ammiel, from Lodebar (2 Samuel 9:1,3-5).

Covenant People Care for the Wounded and Burdened

Now when Mephibosheth, the son of Jonathan, the son of Saul, was come unto David, he fell on his face, and did reverence. And David said, Mephibosheth. And he answered, Behold thy servant!

So Mephibosheth dwelt in Jerusalem: for he did eat continually at the king's table; and was lame on both his feet (2 Samuel 9:6,13).

New Testament Applications

Jesus Was Committed to Our Seed

But when Jesus saw it, He was much displeased, and said unto them, Suffer the little children to come unto Me, and forbid them not: for of such is the kingdom of God (Mark 10:14).

Paul's Commitment to Spiritual Seed

My little children, of whom I travail in birth again until Christ be formed in you (Galatians 4:19).

Chapter Fifteen

Covenant People Are Not Perfect but They Have a Perfect Heart

David has been anything but perfect, yet he has maintained a perfect heart. God never seeks a perfect man, but a man after His own heart (see Acts 13:22). The heart of David is perfectly covenantal. God chooses people who are not perfect. He looks on the heart, discerning motives, not just actions. David *is not perfect, but he has a perfect heart.*

David has made many mistakes in his journey, just as we all have. But, he has never before made such a mistake as he is about to make. For the first time in his life, he is about to step outside of covenant and reveal the awful penalty of living outside the boundaries of those relationships.

Chapter 11 of Second Samuel opens by noting that it was the time when kings go forth to battle. However, David tarried in

Jerusalem. Covenant people should be where they are supposed to be when they are supposed to be there. David stayed at home when he was supposed to be in battle.

The king arose from his bed to take a walk on the roof. While there, he spotted a beautiful woman taking a bath. Upon his inquiry, it was revealed that she was the wife of Uriah the Hittite, and that her name was Bathsheba. The name *Bathsheba* from the Hebrew means "the daughter of an oath"[1]; the "*sheba*" in her name also means "seven."[2]

David sent for this beautiful woman and slept with her, knowing full well that her husband was away at battle. From this illicit affair, Bathsheba conceived. She sent and told David that she was with child—his child. David then commissioned the captain of the army, asking that Uriah be brought home for a visit. David hoped that he would sleep with his wife; then they could cover up their treachery by pretending that the baby was her own husband's. Uriah did come home, but he refused to go to his own house because of his honor for the other men who were away at war. He said it would not be fair for him to have the pleasures of home while the other men were risking their lives (see 2 Sam. 11:11).

David then sent a message to the captain of the host to put Uriah on the forefront of the hottest battle. David had determined that if his plan to cover up the affair would not work, he would have the woman's husband killed. Then he could take her for his own wife. The plan succeeded, and Uriah was killed in battle. Adultery, then murder. David was *not perfect*.

> *And when the mourning was past, David sent and fetched her to his house, and she became his wife, and bare him a son. But the thing that David had done displeased the Lord* (2 Samuel 11:27).

The most interesting phrase in the above verse is that the awful thing that David had done had "displeased the Lord." The Lord was not displeased at the marriage, but He was displeased at the activity that happened outside of covenant. *Bathsheba* repre-sented that which is of the "oath" or the number "seven," repre-senting completion and perfection. It is wrong to be joined to that which is complete or of an oath, if there is no covenant. Sin is what we do outside of covenant. There can be no sin in covenant.

God sent Nathan the prophet to David with a word of rebuke and warning for his actions outside of covenant. Jehovah would punish David openly for what he had done secretly. God agreed to forgive David and spare his life because of the uprightness of David's heart, but the child, the fruit of breaking covenant, would have to die (see 2 Sam. 12:9-15). This proves that covenant people can have *a perfect heart without being perfect.*

David wept and fasted all night in repentance, begging God to spare the life of the child—but to no avail, for the child died. David then arose from the earth and washed, anointed himself, and changed his apparel (see 2 Sam. 12:20). This principle reveals that you can recover from broken covenant, but there are still conse-quences from actions taken outside of covenant.

David was not perfect, but he had a perfect heart. This was proven when he was rebuked and exposed by Nathan the prophet. He took complete and total responsibility for his actions by saying, "I and I alone have sinned" (see 2 Sam. 12:13). He expressed his heart this way in Psalm 51:3-4, "For I acknowledge my transgres-sions: and my sin is ever before me. Against Thee, Thee only, have I sinned, and done this evil in Thy sight: that Thou mightest be jus-tified when Thou speakest, and be clear when Thou judgest." David powerfully demonstrated the pureness of his heart by this further prayer of repentance.

Create in me a clean heart, O God; and renew a right spirit within me. Cast me not away from Thy presence; and take not Thy Holy Spirit from me. Restore unto me the joy of Thy sal-vation; and uphold me with Thy free spirit. Then will I teach transgressors Thy ways; and sinners shall be converted unto Thee (Psalm 51:10-13).

Though he had seriously sinned, David was still a man after God's own heart, a man of covenant. He had failed, but his heart was still quick to repent and to take responsibility. Listen to his words as he continued in Psalm 51:17:

The sacrifices of God are a broken spirit: a broken and a contrite heart, O God, thou wilt not despise.

David was a broken and contrite man. *He was not perfect, but he had a perfect heart.*

We often judge others because of their actions, yet we want others to judge us by our intentions. God honored David's heart even though he punished his actions. They lost the child who was conceived out of covenant to death, but Bathsheba conceived another child—wise Solomon—who inherited the throne, and the Lord loved him (see 2 Sam. 12:24). The difference was covenant. One child was conceived out of covenant; the other was conceived in covenant. The same woman was mother to them both. Sin is living outside of covenant. When lust has conceived, it brings forth sin. Sin, when it is finished, brings forth death (see Jas. 1:15). Righteousness is living inside of covenant. Righteousness brings life.

God already knew what David was capable of doing before he committed sin. Before we fail, the grace of God makes provision and plans for our recovery. In His great redemptive plan, He slew the Lamb before He bruised the man (see Rom. 8:20; Rev. 13:8). God ordained that Solomon would be born. And the wisest of men would be born to the same woman that David had sinned with. Thank God for His amazing grace!

Covenant men and women *do not have to be perfect; they just need a perfect heart.* Don't count this covenant man out. He may have become temporarily distracted, but his heart still beats with covenant. *David had a perfect heart.*

When we first met David, we saw that God was drawn to him because of what was in his heart. The Scripture said, "The Lord seeth not as man seeth; for man looketh on the outward appearance, but the Lord looketh on the heart" (1 Sam. 16:7).

David did not behave wisely with Bathsheba in the beginning, and even had Uriah killed. But his heart was still on the Lord. God knew from the beginning that David was not perfect but chose him anyway. God is not looking for perfect vessels. He is just looking for yielded vessels. *Covenant people are not perfect, but they have a perfect heart.*

※ ⌐ ⌐ ※

The greatest mistake David made was not with Bathsheba. His greatest mistake was staying behind at the time when kings go forth to battle (see 2 Sam. 11:1). When we lag behind in the season when God is saying, "Go forth," we will find ourselves in compromising situations. Had he been at battle doing God's will, he would have never seen Bathsheba bathing, nor would he have had an opportunity to sleep with her. Had he not slept with her, he would not have been driven to have her husband slain.

David is not perfect, but he has a perfect heart. His willingness to take responsibility for his actions and his speedy repentance capture God's merciful attention. David is still a man of covenant!

Endnotes

1. James Strong, *Strong's Exhaustive Concordance of the Bible* (Peabody, MA: Hendrickson Publishers, n.d.), **Bathsheba**, #1339.

2. *Strong's*, **Sheba**, #7651.

Old Testament Covenant Scriptures

When Covenant People Step Out of Covenant, Disaster Results

And it came to pass, after the year was expired, at the time when kings go forth to battle, that David sent Joab, and his servants with him, and all Israel; and they destroyed the children of Ammon, and besieged Rabbah. But David tarried still at Jerusalem.

And it came to pass in an eveningtide, that David arose from off his bed, and walked upon the roof of the king's house: and from the roof he saw a woman washing herself; and the woman was very beautiful to look upon.

And David sent and inquired after the woman. And one said, Is not this Bathsheba, the daughter of Eliam, the wife of Uriah the Hittite?

And David sent messengers, and took her; and she came in unto him, and he lay with her; for she was purified from her uncleanness: and she returned unto her house.

And the woman conceived, and sent and told David, and said, I am with child (2 Samuel 11:1-5).

New Testament Applications

Jesus Considered the Heart

Blessed are the pure in heart: for they shall see God (Matthew 5:8).

Paul Preached That God Looks at the Heart

For ye see your calling, brethren, how that not many wise men after the flesh, not many mighty, not many noble, are called:

But God hath chosen the foolish things of the world to confound the wise; and God hath chosen the weak things of the world to confound the things which are mighty;

And base things of the world, and things which are despised, hath God chosen, yea, and things which are not, to bring to nought things that are:

That no flesh should glory in His presence (1 Corinthians 1:26-29).

Chapter Sixteen

Covenant People Will Suffer, but They Will Recover

David is forgiven. Yet we do not insinuate that there are no consequences to the breaking of covenant. His one trip outside of covenant has planted seeds that will produce weeds in his garden for years to come. *He will suffer for his broken covenants.*

Sin will take you farther than you want to go, keep you longer than you want to stay, and cost you more than you are willing to pay. Its penalty is just not worth it.

Nathan the prophet comes to David in Chapter 12 of Second Samuel and says, "You are that man. You are the one who took Bathsheba, and you are the one who had Uriah killed. You are the one who was at home when you should have been at battle. You are a guilty man."

David responds with, "I have sinned; I and I alone." God forgives him immediately, but that does not end the consequences of his actions. He will now have to *suffer the loss of the child* produced by this relationship built on deception. Nothing we produce out of covenant will live.

David and Bathsheba's first child dies, but *they recover with a second child.* They name the second child Solomon, and he is loved of the Lord (see 2 Sam. 12:24). David nicknames the new baby Jedidiah, meaning "Beloved of Jehovah" (see 2 Sam. 12:25). Same woman, different child; one is in the boundaries of covenant and blessed—the other was outside of covenant and had to die.

> *Now therefore the sword shall never depart from thine house; because thou hast despised Me, and hast taken the wife of Uriah the Hittite to be thy wife. Thus saith the Lord, Behold, I will raise up evil against thee out of thine own house, and I will take thy wives before thine eyes, and give them unto thy neighbour, and he shall lie with thy wives in the sight of this sun* (2 Samuel 12:10-11).

Gain and loss have been no stranger in the life of David, but he has not yet *suffered* from within the way he is about to *suffer.* Make no mistake; he will *recover.* But his *recovery* will come with an expensive price tag.

Nathan prophesied that the sword would never depart from David's house—that God would raise up evil against him out of his own house. The Living Bible records in Second Samuel 12:10 that David would have to live under "constant threat" in his own house. Broken covenants create suspicion, distrust, and hatred. Can you imagine all of these in your own home?

A broken covenant had already produced the death of a child. Then David's lust had multiplied itself, invading the palace of the king. Amnon, the son of David, had fallen in love with Tamar, the daughter of David. Amnon pretended to be sick to entice Tamar to care for him, and then he forced her to sleep with him (see 2 Sam. 13:14).

Lust had given way to rape, and rape had given way to hate (see 2 Sam. 13:15). After he had his way with Tamar, Amnon's hatred of her exceeded his previous love for her. Sin will always use and abuse you, then throw you away. All these things were the consequences of a broken covenant. God has provided for our every need inside of covenant relationships. We should never go outside of those boundaries.

Tamar in her humiliation went to her full blood brother and told him what had happened to her by their half brother. Absalom hated Amnon from that day forward and began to plot his death (see 2 Sam. 13:20,22). Hatred was in full bloom in the palace of the king. These two brothers did not speak to each other for two full years, and all of this was going on in the king's house.

David became so preoccupied with his failure that he lost sight of the problems among his own children. His only response to his own daughter's rape is recorded in Second Samuel 13:21:

But when King David heard of all these things, he was very wroth.

That's it. That was all that was said of his reaction. He was angry! What disasters a broken covenant can bring to a household.

Absalom finally manipulated David into allowing all his sons to go sheep shearing together. While they were all away, Absalom had Amnon killed in revenge (see 2 Sam. 13:28-29). Do you remember Uriah? Nathan had warned, "The sword will not depart from the house of David." Had David been aware of what was going on in his own house, he would have known these boys had become enemies.

So Absalom fled, and went to Geshur, and was there three years. And the soul of king David longed to go forth unto Absalom: for he was comforted concerning Amnon, seeing he was dead (2 Samuel 13:38-39).

The Power of a Covenant Heart

By this time, David regretted the day he went walking on the roof when he should have gone off to battle. It would have been much easier to battle "giants from without" than to have to live with these "giants from within."

Absalom did return to Jerusalem, but not as a humbled servant. He returned as a polished politician with a very personal agenda to steal the throne from his father. One broken covenant had created death, lust, rape, hatred, murder, and then religious politics.

Absalom was so very attractive with much natural charisma. His beautiful hair caused all the people to praise him (see 2 Sam. 14:25-26). His pride soon got the best of him as he began his campaign to win the support of the people. When the people came to David for counsel, Prince Absalom caught them at the gate, greeted them, shook hands, and kissed them (see 2 Sam. 15:2-6). As a slick politician, Absalom won the hearts of the people.

And there came a messenger to David, saying, The hearts of the men of Israel are after Absalom (2 Samuel 15:13).

David, still operating under the guilt of his personal moral failures, abdicated the throne and ran for his life from his own son (see 2 Sam. 15:14). Sin always brings consequences. David's sin caused him *to suffer*, but it was his condemnation and guilt that continued to plague him. *He needed to recover.*

Feeling abandoned and all alone, David was licking his wounds. When he came to Bahurim, Shimei came out, cursing and spitting, even throwing rocks at him. The men with David sought to silence and even kill this accuser, but David was having a pity party and told them to let the man continue to taunt him (see 2 Sam. 16:9-13). *Shimei* is derived from a Hebrew word that means "rumors or things heard." David was being cursed, spit on, and assaulted by rumors. If he did not recover in a hurry, his guilt would kill him before Absalom even had a chance.

Guilt had created an atmosphere for sin to repeat itself. Absalom then went up on the roof and slept with his father's concubines. The iniquity of the father was visiting a new generation in the same location (see 2 Sam. 16:22)! While all of this had been going on, David had reckoned the matter finished, and thereby *he had recovered* (see 2 Sam. 15:30-37). David then sent Hushai as a spy into Absalom's camp.

In the meantime, Absalom was "feeling his oats." His rebellious conceit was at an all-time high. He heeded the counsel of Hushai as *God began the recovery* (see 2 Sam. 17:14). As Absalom rode high on his pride, with his hair flowing in the wind, he was caught by a limb of a great oak tree and snatched from his mule by the hair of his head. His own self-importance had snared him (see 2 Sam. 18:9-10). His pride preceded his fall (see Prov. 16:18). Joab passed by and killed him there hanging in the tree by his hair (see 2 Sam. 18:14-18).

David received a message from Cushi that Absalom was dead. Cushi was a man running with a true message for the king. Many today try to weaken what it is to be a Cushite by making it only a racial issue. There are not enough Cushites today. Anyone of any race or gender that is running with a true message that moves the heart of the King qualifies as a Cushite, regardless of skin color.

* * *

The *suffering* of David has come full circle. He has lost a baby, incest has invaded the palace, hatred and murder have prevailed in his own home, and Absalom has slept with his concubines on the same roof where it all began. Joab has murdered Absalom. As Nathan had prophesied, the sword has not departed from David's house. David weeps and weeps for Absalom and for what broken covenant has produced in his family (see 2 Sam. 19:4). David *has endured suffering, but he will recover.*

In fact, David leads a victorious campaign against the brothers of Goliath and kills them all (see 2 Sam. 21:15-22). After his victory over the giants from within, he feels the need to conquer the remaining giants from without. Then David sings praises for two more chapters (see 2 Sam. 22–23). *He has endured suffering, but he has recovered.* If it happened for David, it can happen for you.

Recovery is not so much about getting everything back as it is about becoming covered again. *Re* means "once again," while *cover* means "to shield or to protect; to keep warm." *Suffering* often makes us aware of our need for and appreciation of *covering. Covenant people do suffer, but they do recover.*

Old Testament Covenant Scriptures

Covenant Breaking Affects Family Relarionships

But when king David heard of all these things, he was very wroth.

Then the king arose, and tare his garments, and lay on the earth; and all his servants stood by with their clothes rent.

...And David mourned for his son every day.

And the soul of king David longed to go forth unto Absalom: for he was comforted concerning Amnon, seeing he was dead (2 Samuel 13:21,31,37,39).

But in all Israel there was none to be so much praised as Absalom for his beauty: from the sole of his foot even to the crown of his head there was no blemish in him.

So Absalom dwelt two full years in Jerusalem, and saw not the king's face.

...and the king kissed Absalom (2 Samuel 14:25,28,33).

Covenant Breaking Often Carries Lifelong Consequences

And on this manner did Absalom to all Israel that came to the king for judgment: so Absalom stole the hearts of the men of Israel.

And there came a messenger to David, saying, The hearts of the men of Israel are after Absalom (2 Samuel 15:6,13).

And Absalom and all the men of Israel said, The counsel of Hushai the Archite is better than the counsel of Ahithophel. For the Lord had appointed to defeat the good counsel of Ahithophel, to the intent that the Lord might bring evil upon Absalom (2 Samuel 17:14).

And a certain man saw it, and told Joab, and said, Behold, I saw Absalom hanged in an oak.

And the king was much moved, and went up to the chamber over the gate, and wept: and as he went, thus he said, O my son Absalom, my son, my son Absalom! would God I had died for thee, O Absalom, my son, my son! (2 Samuel 18:10,33)

But the king covered his face, and the king cried with a loud voice, O my son Absalom, O Absalom, my son, my son! (2 Samuel 19:4)

New Testament Applications

Jesus Overcame Sufferings

These things I have spoken unto you, that in Me ye might have peace. In the world ye shall have tribulation: but be of good cheer; I have overcome the world (John 16:33).

Though He were a Son, yet learned He obedience by the things which He suffered (Hebrews 5:8).

Paul Taught That We Would Recover From Sufferings

For I reckon that the sufferings of this present time are not worthy to be compared with the glory which shall be revealed in us (Romans 8:18).

Chapter Seventeen

Covenant People Are Multigenerational

The power of a covenant heart is difficult for many to understand, because it transcends generational barriers. David began his covenant with Jonathan by extending it to their seed after them. This covenant philosophy must outlive those of us who proclaim it. Our message must be *multigenerational*. The Kingdom of God and the power of a covenant heart will always be relevant to every generation.

Jesus went from talking to lawyers and Pharisees to holding children in his lap and comparing them to the Kingdom of God. His reason was most relevant. Covenant is a message to and for every generation. The church with no relevant message for each and every generation is a dying church.

After David becomes old and well stricken in age, one of his sons, Adonijah, exalts himself and seeks to be king (see 1 Kings 1:5). Bathsheba reminds David of his covenant with her that Solomon will rule in his stead (see 1 Kings 1:17). If David does not choose and anoint a successor, then Adonijah will continue to reign after him.

David understood what few today understand—you don't have a right to die until you place your mantle on another generation! David is a man with a covenant heart. *Covenant people are multigenerational.*

❊ ⸺ ❊

David summoned the priest and the prophet to prepare for the coronation of a new king. It was no accident that the king chose a priest and a prophet to assist in the ordination. David had always demonstrated a threefold anointing of prophet, priest, and king. David was a beautiful picture of our Prophet, Priest, and King—Jesus Christ, our great High King Priest after the order of Melchisedec (see 1 Kings 1:34; Heb. 5:1–8:6).

One of the wealthiest places on our planet is the local grave-yard, because buried there is a vast treasury of wisdom, dreams, visions, and even anointings that were never imparted to another generation. Covenant people do not have the right to carry their anointing with them to Heaven. You should not die, unless you die empty! Pour it out! *Covenant people are multigenerational.*

David did not wait until after his death to give his blessing and impartation to another generation. He took action while he was alive to ensure the continuity of vision and purpose. Too often vision is lost because of the lack of impartation from one generation to another.

Each covenant man or woman alive today on planet earth has an obligation to transfer his vision, insight, and anointing to the next generation. Again, you should not die until you are empty. God has given you a purpose, and that purpose is not complete until the next generation can run with your vision to take it to the next level. If you have not emptied yourself into someone else, you should not die yet. If you go to Heaven with your vision and purpose, then you are an intruder there.

David did not die until he anointed, consecrated, ordained, and charged Solomon to carry on in his stead. Take the time to read First Kings 2:1-10. Our covenant will outlast our days on this planet. God is multigenerational. *Covenant people are multigenerational.* Your seed may be chosen to finish your vision, but they cannot do that if you take it with you to Heaven.

Every Old Testament patriarch refused to die until he passed his mantle to another generation—Abraham to Isaac, Isaac to Jacob, Israel to Ephraim and Manasseh. *The multigenerational blessing was always released before death.*

Moses did not die until he charged and prepared Joshua. Elijah was only free to go after he cast his mantle on Elisha. Jesus appeared to His disciples with instructions before ascending. From the Old Testament to the New Testament, God's chosen vessels were required to pass their anointing on to the next generation. We must stop allowing the truth of one generation to die with that generation. *Covenant people are multigenerational.*

In the New Testament, the Apostle Paul stated in Second Timothy 4:6 that he was ready to depart. He had fought a good fight and had kept the faith. He knew there was a crown of righteousness laid up for him, but that did not give him the right to die. He had not yet cast his mantle.

He called for his son in the Lord, Timothy, and told him to come to him quickly (see 2 Tim. 4:9). Paul was sitting all alone in a dark, dirty prison cell. He was lonely and cold. He was ready to depart, but he could not until he cast his cloak on another generation.

Paul told Timothy to come before winter, and "when you come, go by Troas, pick up my cloak that I left with Carpus, and bring it with you." He also told him to bring with him the books that he had written and especially the parchments he had been working on just before he was jailed (see 2 Tim. 4:13,21).

Paul understood as did David, that *covenant people are multigenerational.* He knew that fighting a good fight and keeping the faith was not permission to die. You cannot die until you cast your mantle.

Paul said the season was changing, and he instructed Timothy to come see him before winter. He asked for the books, but especially the parchments, because there were things written that he needed to explain to Timothy before he could depart. He was preparing to cast his cloak on Timothy. Timothy represented the next generation of leadership, Paul the previous generation. This covenant must go from generation to generation.

David was described in the first chapter of First Kings as not being able to stay warm, but he could not die until he anointed Solomon. Second Timothy chapter 4 describes Paul as being in the winter looking for his cloak, but he could not die until Timothy came to him with the books, parchments, and the cloak. *Covenant people are multigenerational.*

We have lost too many valuable resources to the grave by not passing them on to another generation. Malachi promised that the heart of the fathers would be turned to the children, and the heart of the children would be turned to the fathers (see Mal. 4:6). That means the day is upon us when we will not lose our greatest resources when covenant people die, because they will pass their gift on to another generation.

> *And Abraham gave all that he had unto Isaac... Then Abraham gave up the ghost, and died in a good old age, an old man, and full of years; and was gathered to his people* (Genesis 25:5,8).

Until you have given all that you have to another generation, you should not give up the ghost. Again, you should not die before your time. If you do you will go to Heaven as an intruder. Abraham was empty, old, and full of years. That is the biblical pattern on the way to die.

In Genesis chapters 27-28, Isaac blessed and charged Jacob. In Genesis chapter 48, Jacob was sick and dying, yet he could not die until he saw his grandchildren to bless them and impart into them. The promise of another generation caused a weak, sick, old man named Jacob to strengthen himself and become Israel (see Gen. 48:2). Don't die weak and feeble; strengthen yourself and impart to the next generation. *Covenant people are multigenerational.*

Moses did not die until he laid his hands upon Joshua (see Deut. 34:9). The Scripture says that the people listened to Joshua as they would have Moses, because of the impartation from one generation to another. That is why so many ministries fold with the death of the visionary. There is no multigenerational vision. *We must pass the vision on to another generation.*

David did not die until he installed Solomon as king in his stead. He charged Solomon to be strong and show himself a man. Then and only then did he go to sleep with his fathers and was buried (see 1 Kings 2:10).

In Second Kings chapter 2, Elijah was not taken up in the whirlwind until Elisha was promised the mantle. Elisha received it and operated in double strength authority because of the power of impartation. The time is now for a double portion generation to operate under the power of a covenant heart. Elisha sought and received a double portion of the spirit of Elijah. In Genesis chapter 48, Ephraim received the right hand blessing from Israel; Ephraim's name meant "double fruitfulness." Double fruit and double portions are obtained only by impartation through covenant relationships.

Jesus did not ascend until He gathered together His apostles and gave them commandments and taught them about the Kingdom of God. He then instructed them to tarry in Jerusalem until they received the mantle of the Holy Ghost. Then He departed out of their sight and was received up into Heaven (see Acts 1:2-9). Not even Jesus was free to depart until He passed His vision and anointing on to another generation. *Covenant people are multigenerational!*

Old Testament Covenant Scriptures

Covenant People Pass on Their Legacy

Now king David was old and stricken in years; and they covered him with clothes, but he gat no heat.

And Bathsheba bowed, and did obeisance unto the king. And the king said, What wouldest thou?

And she said unto him, My lord, thou swarest by the Lord thy God unto thine handmaid, saying, Assuredly Solomon thy son shall reign after me, and he shall sit upon my throne.

Then king David answered and said, Call me Bathsheba. And she came into the king's presence, and stood before the king.

And the king sware, and said, As the Lord liveth, that hath redeemed my soul out of all distress,

Even as I sware unto thee by the Lord God of Israel, saying, Assuredly Solomon thy son shall reign after me, and he shall sit upon my throne in my stead; even so will I certainly do this day.

And Zadok the priest took an horn of oil out of the tabernacle, and anointed Solomon. And they blew the trumpet; and all the people said, God save king Solomon.

And all the people came up after him, and the people piped with pipes, and rejoiced with great joy, so that the earth rent with the sound of them.

And also Solomon sitteth on the throne of the kingdom (1 Kings 1:1,16-17,28-30,39-40,46).

Now the days of David drew nigh that he should die; and he charged Solomon his son, saying, I go the way of all the earth: be thou strong therefore, and show thyself a man (1 Kings 2:1-2).

New Testament Applications

Jesus Was Multigenerational

Verily, verily, I say unto you, Except a corn of wheat fall into the ground and die, it abideth alone: but if it die, it bringeth forth much fruit (John 12:24).

Yet it pleased the Lord to bruise Him; He hath put Him to grief: when Thou shalt make His soul an offering for sin, He shall see His seed, He shall prolong His days, and the pleasure of the Lord shall prosper in His hand (Isaiah 53:10).

And again, I will put my trust in Him. And again, Behold I and the children which God hath given me (Hebrews 2:13).

Paul Recognized Multigenerational Blessings

When I call to remembrance the unfeigned faith that is in thee, which dwelt first in thy grandmother Lois, and thy mother Eunice; and I am persuaded that in thee also (2 Timothy 1:5).

Conclusion

Now that you have journeyed with David and read his story, the vision is clear. Our final point is the most powerful one. You do not have a right to die with your vision and anointing. It must be passed on to another generation. Any vision that is small enough for you to finish by yourself is too small. You need a covenant vision, not a dispensational one. *Covenant vision will go from generation to generation.* A true prophetic vision will be larger than one generation.

David is the pattern and prototype of the covenant heart. By the power of a covenant heart, get up, get busy, and pass your dreams, visions, and anointing on to another generation. By the grace of God, we will not lose the treasures when we put off these earthen vessels. From this day forward, we must empty ourselves into those who will come behind us.

From his days in the field as a shepherd boy until his burial in the city of David, the sweet psalmist of Israel shows us *The Power of a Covenant Heart.* Each step David takes is a learning experience, yet it is his final action from which we learn the most. Pass your mantle on to the next generation, and you will live on forever through them. Refuse to die. Live on by passing the faith along.

The Power of a Covenant Heart is the power of an endless life. David still lives because he is still speaking to you and me. Will we continue to speak after we have been buried? The answer will be determined by what we do while we are alive.

Let our vision be multigenerational. Be ambitious for your seed and your seed's seed. They are to far exceed anything that you and I will live to accomplish by ourselves. If we do our job correctly, we will live on and accomplish greater exploits through them. May *the Power of a Covenant Heart* live on for thousands of generations!

Additional copies of this book and other
book titles from DESTINY IMAGE are
available at your local bookstore.

For a complete list of our titles,
visit us at www.destinyimage.com
Send a request for a catalog to:

Destiny Image® Publishers, Inc.

P.O. Box 310
Shippensburg, PA 17257-0310

*"Speaking to the Purposes of God for This
Generation and for the Generations to Come"*